The Best of Merle Haggard

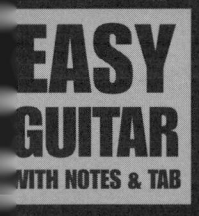

EASY GUITAR WITH NOTES & TAB

2 Strum and Pick Patterns

3   Are the Good Times Really Over for Good
6   Big City
8   Blue Jungle
11 Carolyn
14 The Emptiest Arms in the World
20 From Graceland to the Promised Land
17 I Had a Beautiful Time
22 I Started Loving You Again
24 I Think I'll Just Stay Here and Drink
26 If We Make It Through December
28 It's Been a Great Afternoon
30 Let's Chase Each Other Around the Room
32 Mama Tried
35 Misery and Gin
38 My Favorite Memory
44 Okie From Muskogee
46 A Place to Fall Apart
41 Rainbow Stew
48 Ramblin' Fever
52 Reasons to Quit
54 Red Bandana
56 Sing Me Back Home
62 Twinkle Twinkle Lucky Star
58 Workin' Man Blues
60 You Take Me for Granted

ISBN 978-0-634-01046-0

HAL•LEONARD® CORPORATION
7777 W. BLUEMOUND RD. P.O. BOX 13819 MILWAUKEE, WI 53213

For all works contained herein:
Unauthorized copying, arranging, adapting, recording or public performance is an infringement of copyright.
Infringers are liable under th

Visit Hal Leonard Online at
www.halleonard.com

STRUM AND PICK PATTERNS

This chart contains the suggested strum and pick patterns that are referred to by number at the beginning of each song in this book. The symbols ⊓ and ∨ in the strum patterns refer to down and up strokes, respectively. The letters in the pick patterns indicate which right-hand fingers plays which strings.

p = thumb
i = index finger
m = middle finger
a = ring finger

For example; Pick Pattern 2
is played: thumb - index - middle - ring

Strum Patterns / Pick Patterns

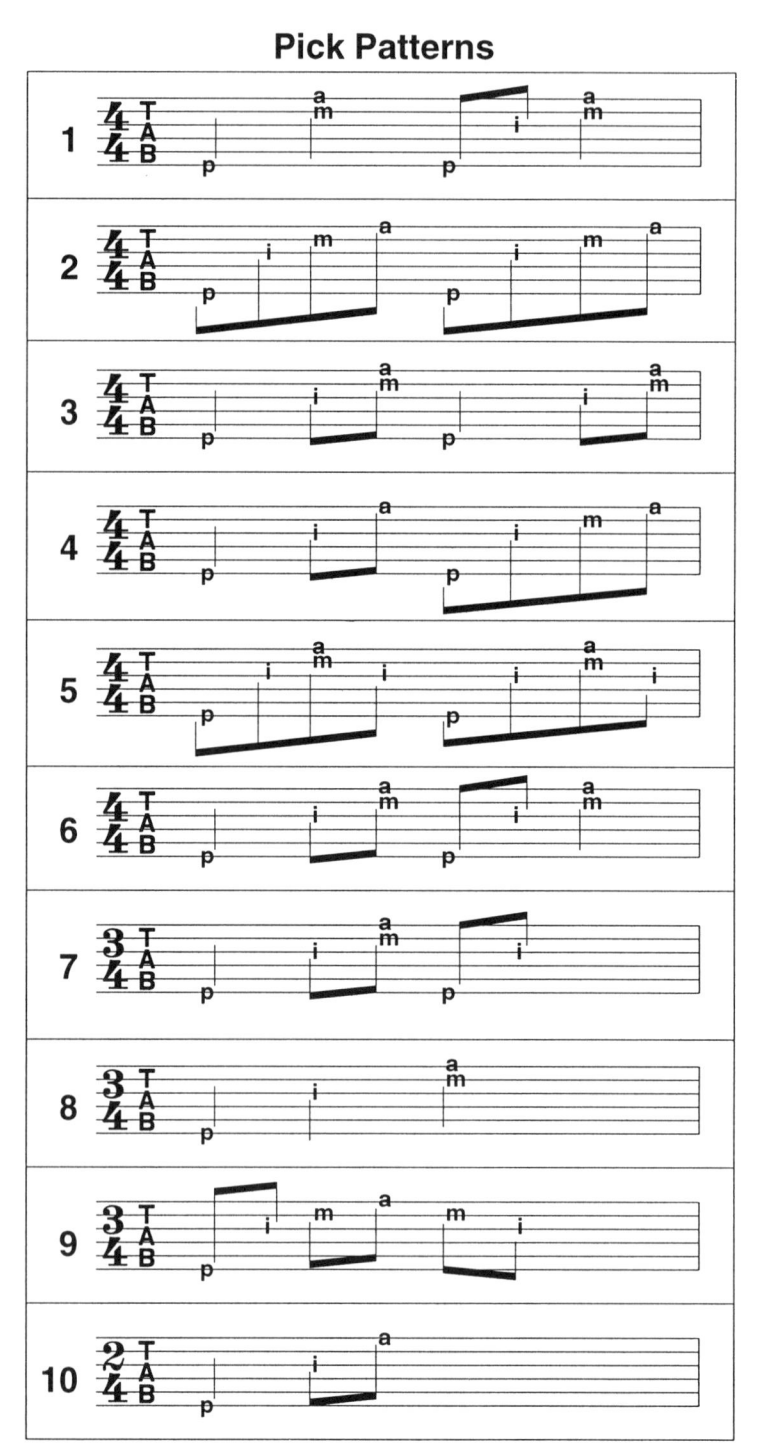

You can use the 3/4 Strum or Pick Patterns in songs written in compound meter (6/8, 9/8, 12/8, etc.). For example, you can accompany a song in 6/8 by playing the 3/4 pattern twice in each measure. The 4/4 Strum and Pick Patterns can be used for songs written in cut time (¢) by doubling the note time values in the patterns. Each pattern would therefore last two measures in cut time.

Are the Good Times Really Over for Good

Words and Music by Merle Haggard

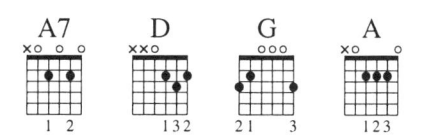

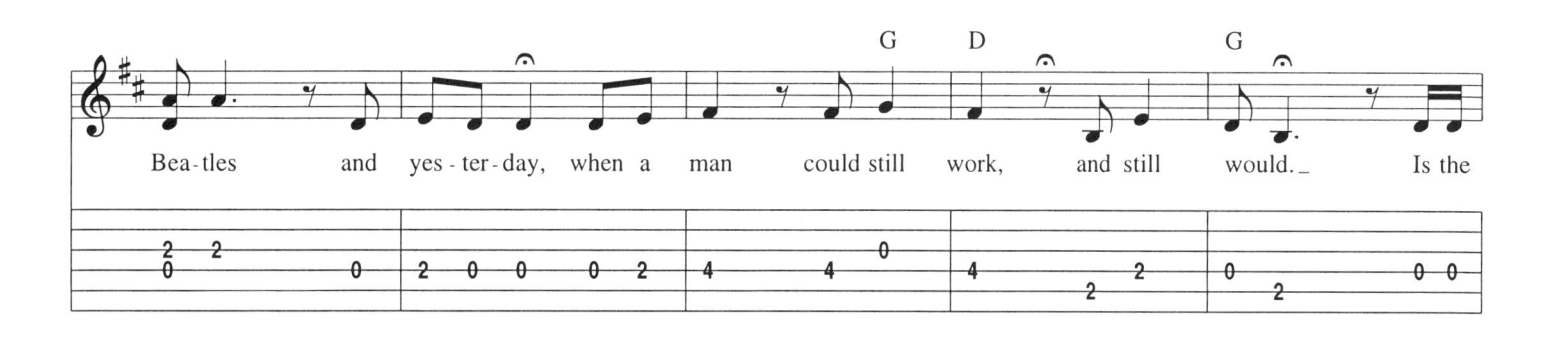

A7 D G A

Strum Pattern: 8, 9
Pick Pattern: 8, 9

Intro
Slowly

1. I wish a

Verse

buck was still sil - ver, and it was back when the coun - try was strong,
2. *See Additional Lyrics*

back be - fore El - vis, and be - fore the Vi - et - nam war came a - long. Be - fore the

Bea - tles and yes - ter - day, when a man could still work, and still would. Is the

Copyright © 1981 Sony/ATV Songs LLC
All Rights Administered by Sony/ATV Music Publishing, 8 Music Square West, Nashville, TN 37203
International Copyright Secured   All Rights Reserved

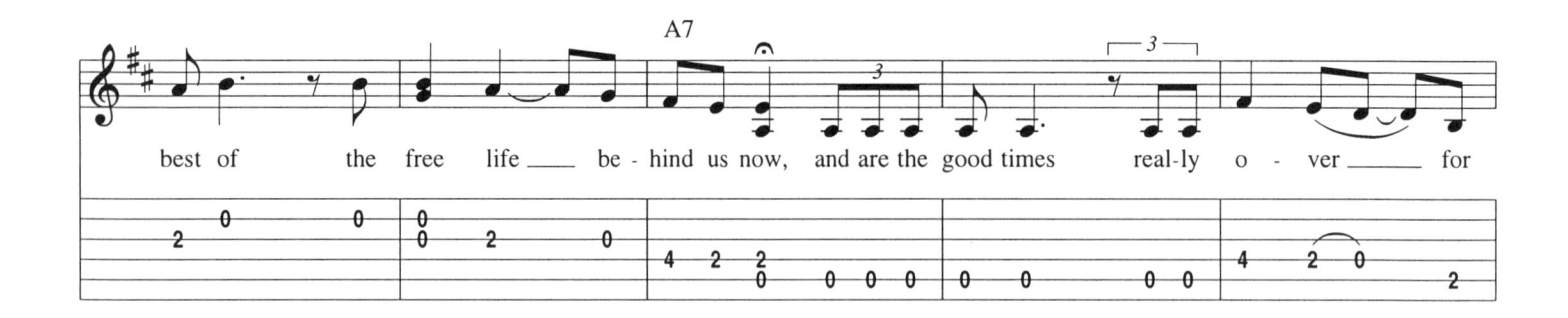

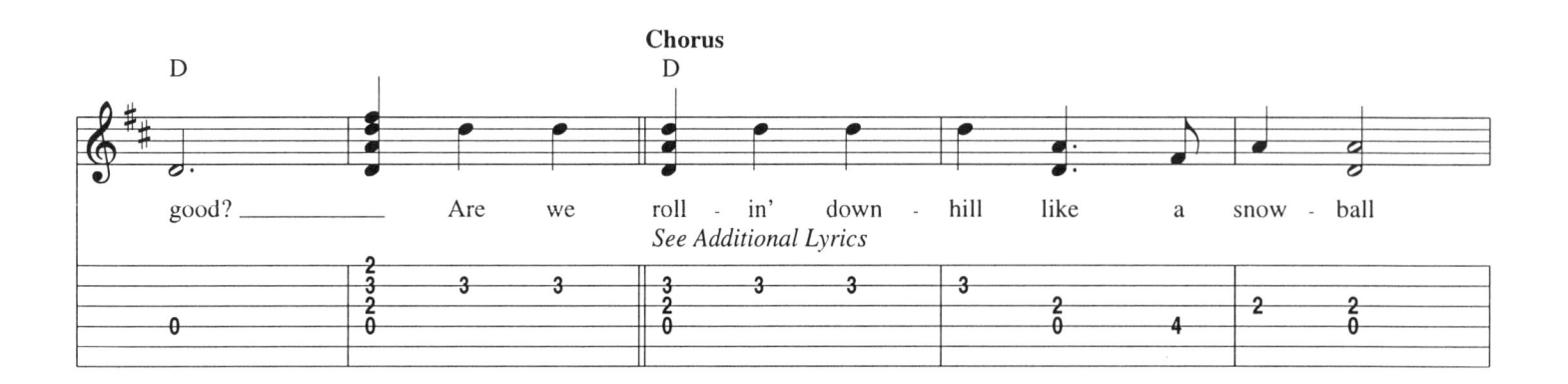

best of the free life ____ be-hind us now, and are the good times real-ly o-ver ____ for

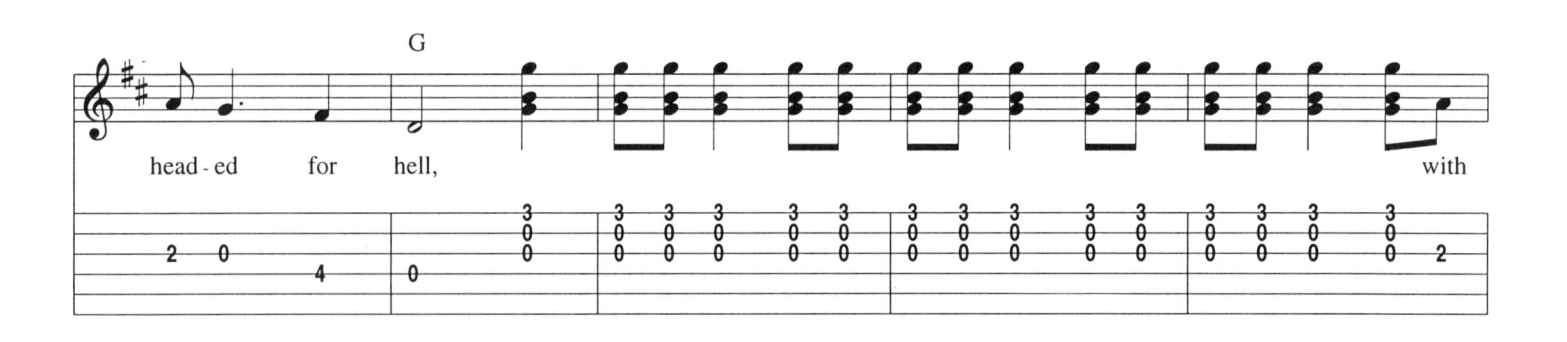

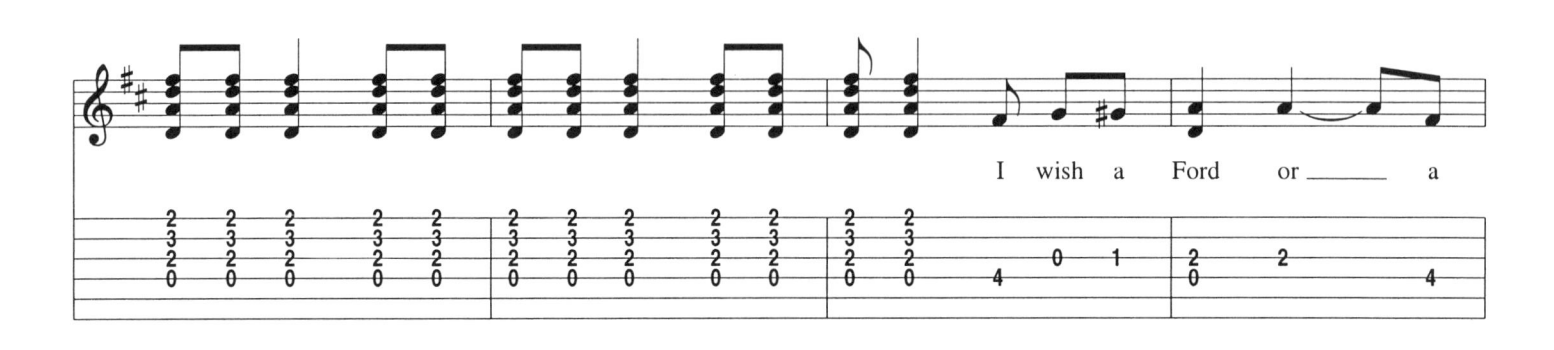

good? ____ Are we rollin' down-hill like a snow-ball
See Additional Lyrics

head-ed for hell, with

no kind ____ of chance ____ for the flag or the lib-er-ty bell? ____

I wish a Ford or ____ a

Additional Lyrics

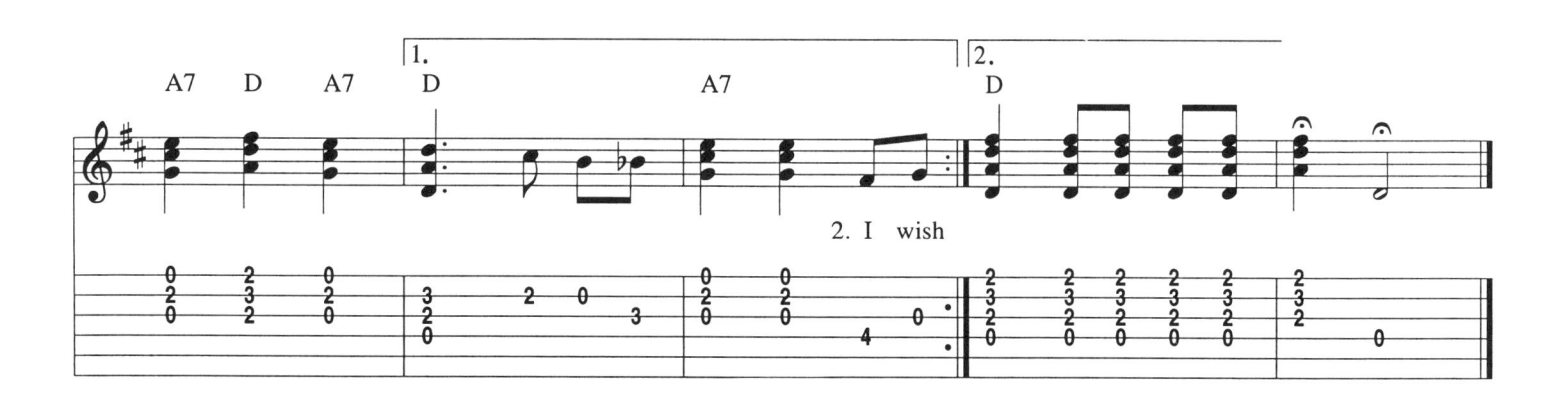

2. I wish coke was still cola,
And a joint was a bad place to be.
It was back before Nixon lied to us all on TV.
Before microwave ovens,
When a girl could still cook,
And still would.

Chorus Is the best of the free life behind us now,
And are the good times really over for good?
Stop rollin' downhill like a snowball headed for hell,
Stand up for the flag, and let's all ring the liberty bell.
Let's make a Ford and a Chevy
That'll still last ten years like they should.
The best of the free life is still yet to come,
And the good times ain't over for good.

Big City

Words and Music by Merle Haggard and Dean Holloway

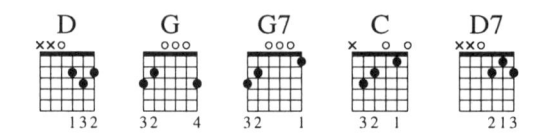

Chords: D, G, G7, C, D7

Strum Pattern: 4, 6
Pick Pattern: 3, 4

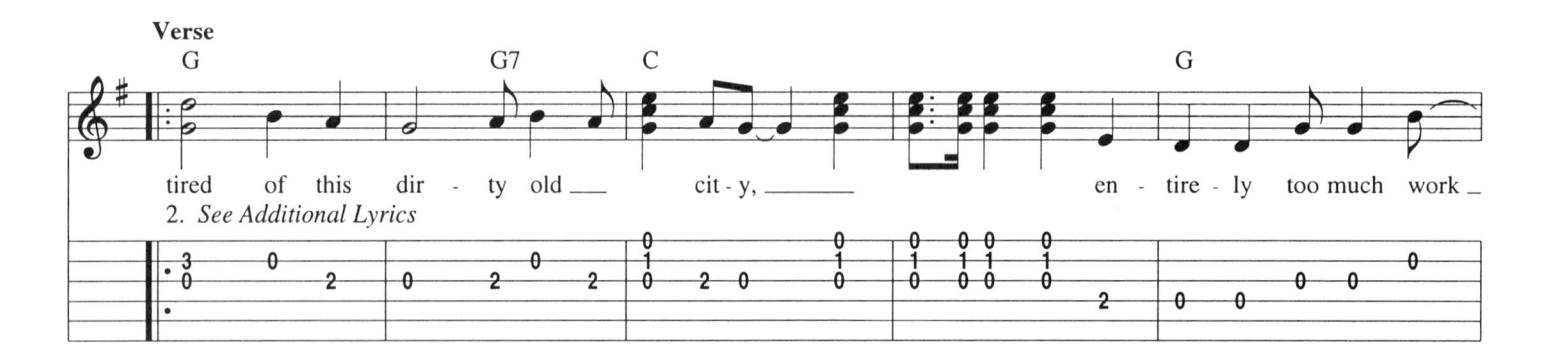

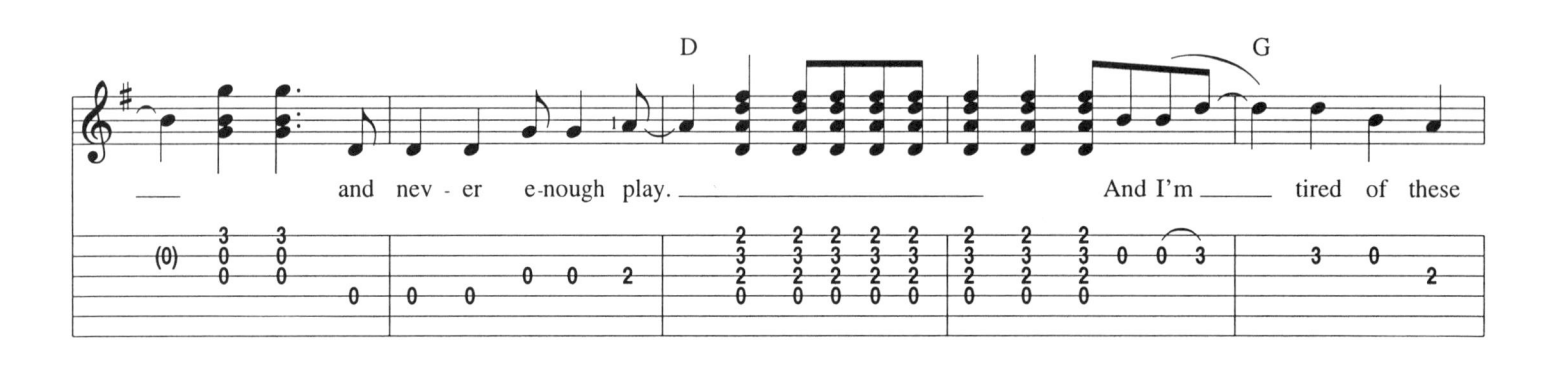

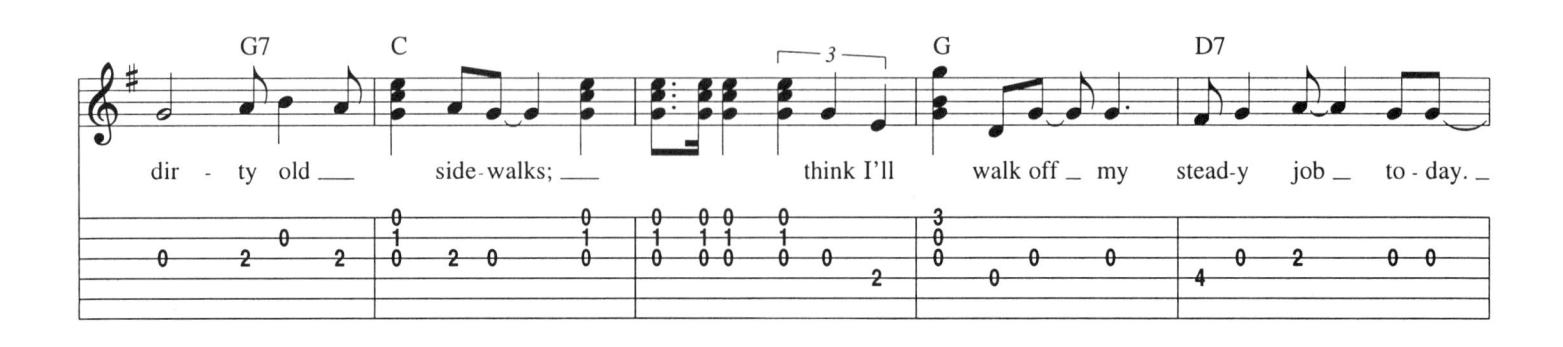

Intro
Reflectively

Verse

1. I'm tired of this dirty old city, entirely too much work and never enough play. And I'm tired of these dirty old sidewalks; think I'll walk off my steady job today.

2. *See Additional Lyrics*

Copyright © 1981 Sony/ATV Songs LLC
All Rights Administered by Sony/ATV Music Publishing, 8 Music Square West, Nashville, TN 37203
International Copyright Secured   All Rights Reserved

Chorus

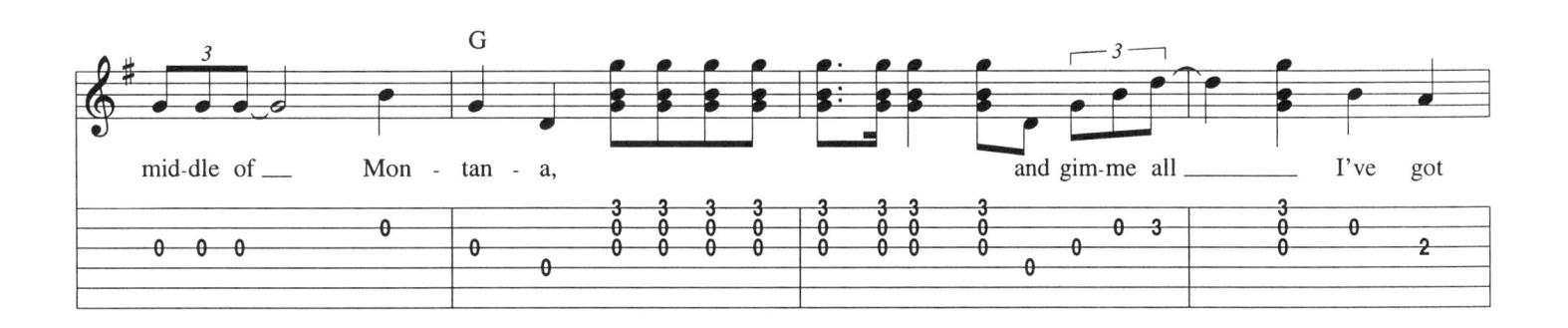

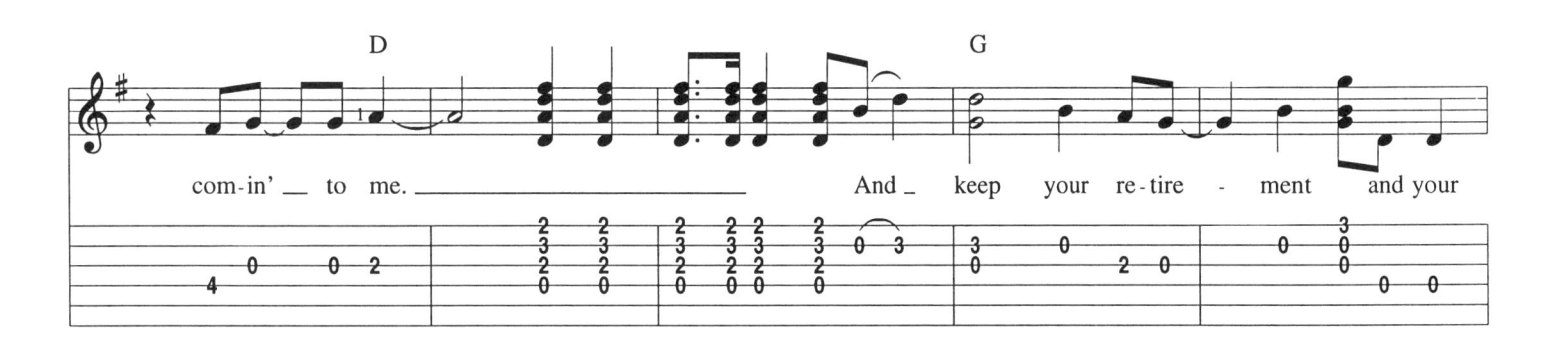

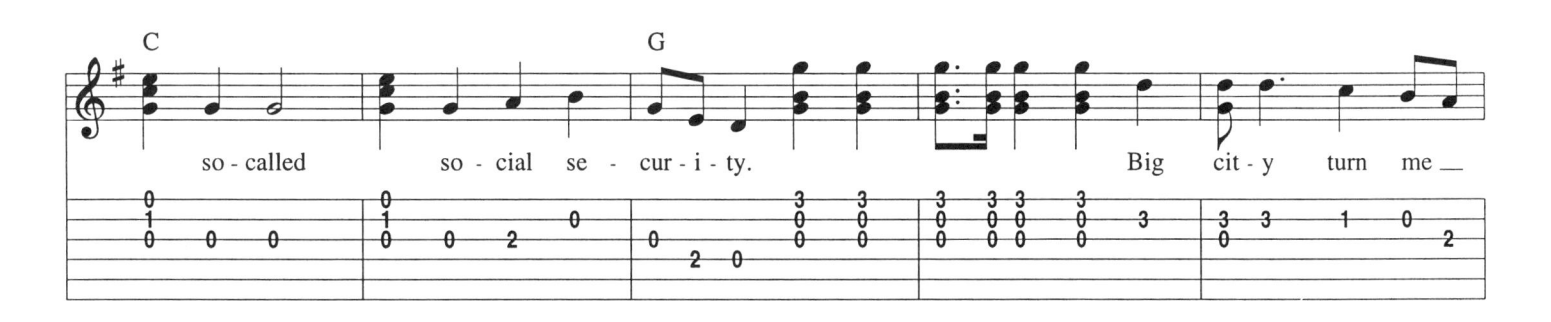

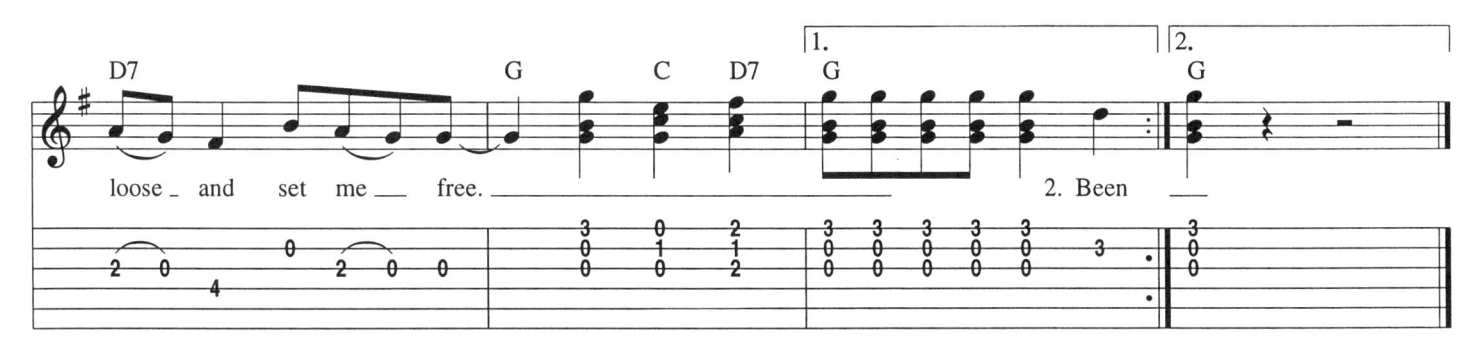

Turn me loose, set me free, somewhere in the middle of Montana, and gimme all I've got comin' to me. And keep your retirement and your so-called social security. Big city turn me loose and set me free.

Additional Lyrics

2. Been workin' ev'ryday since I was twenty,
   Haven't got a thing to show for anything I've done.
   There's folks who never work and they've got plenty;
   Think it's time some guys like me had some fun.

Blue Jungle

Words and Music by Merle Haggard and Freddy Powers

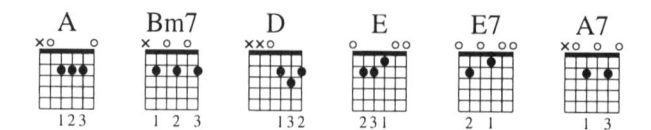

Strum Pattern: 2, 3
Pick Pattern: 3, 4

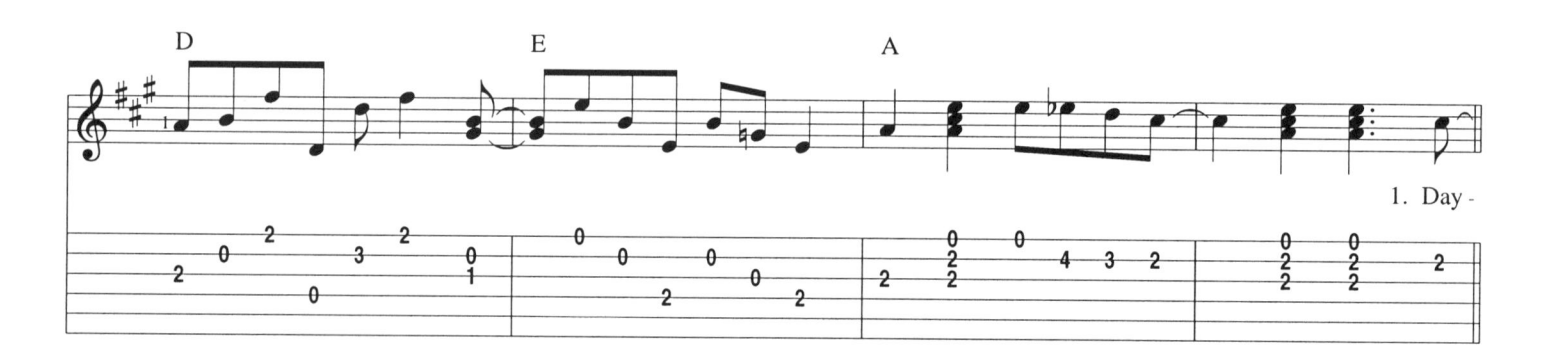

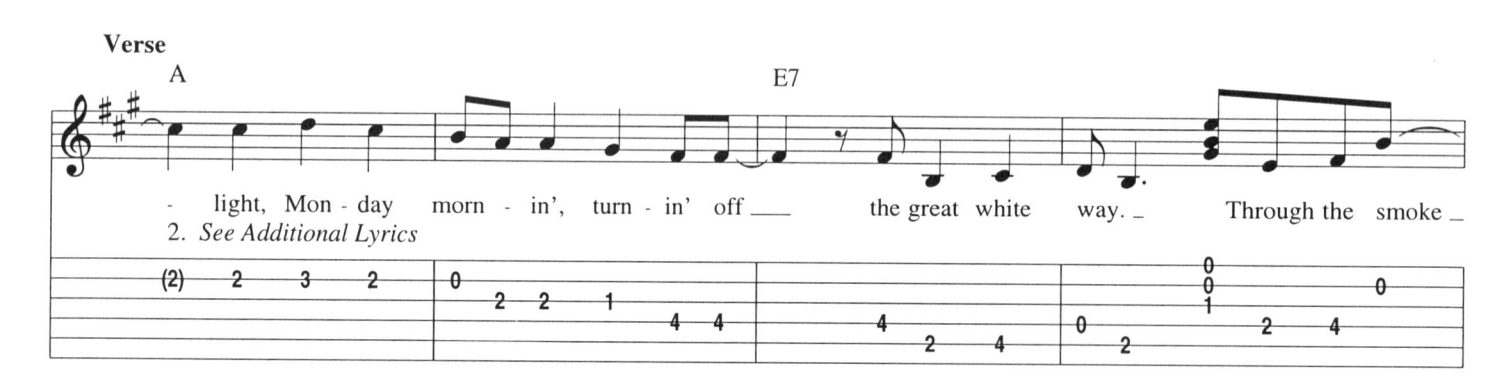

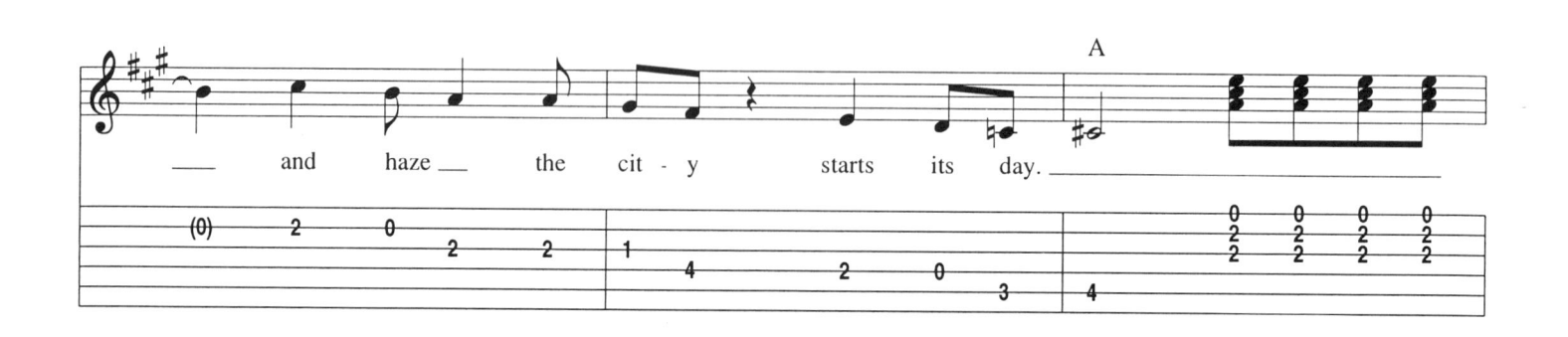

Intro
Bright Country

1. Day-light, Monday mornin', turnin' off the great white way. Through the smoke
2. See Additional Lyrics

and haze the city starts its day.

Copyright © 1990 Sony/ATV Songs LLC
All Rights Administered by Sony/ATV Music Publishing, 8 Music Square West, Nashville, TN 37203
International Copyright Secured All Rights Reserved

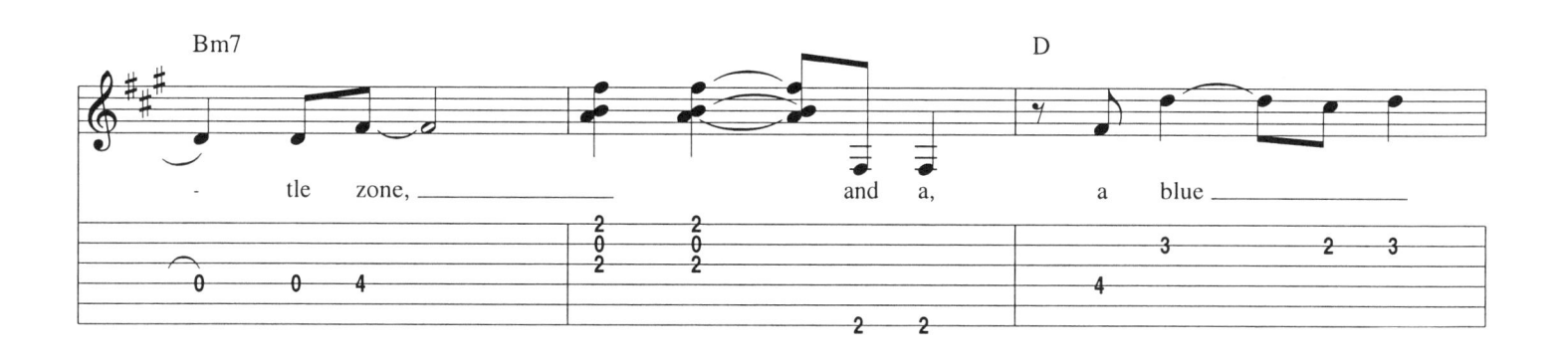

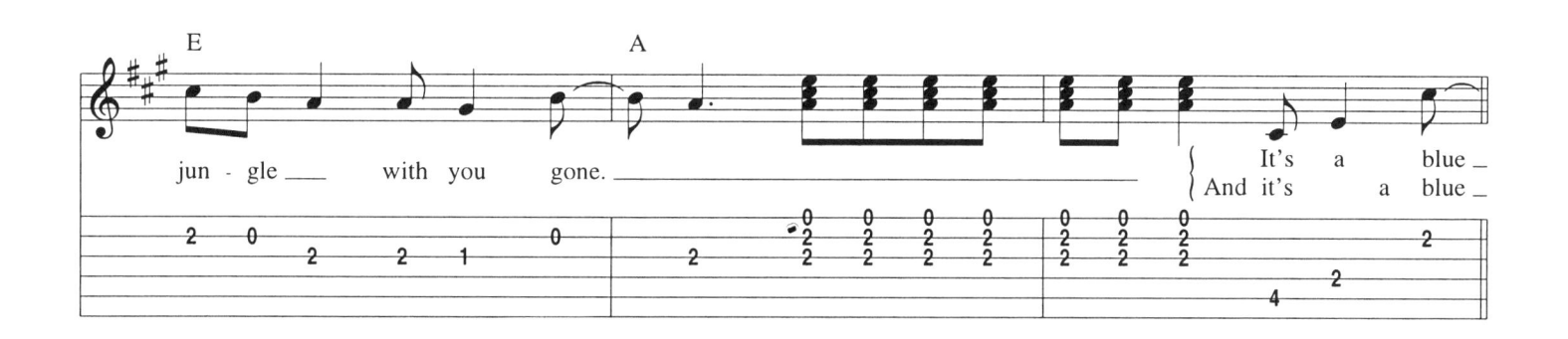

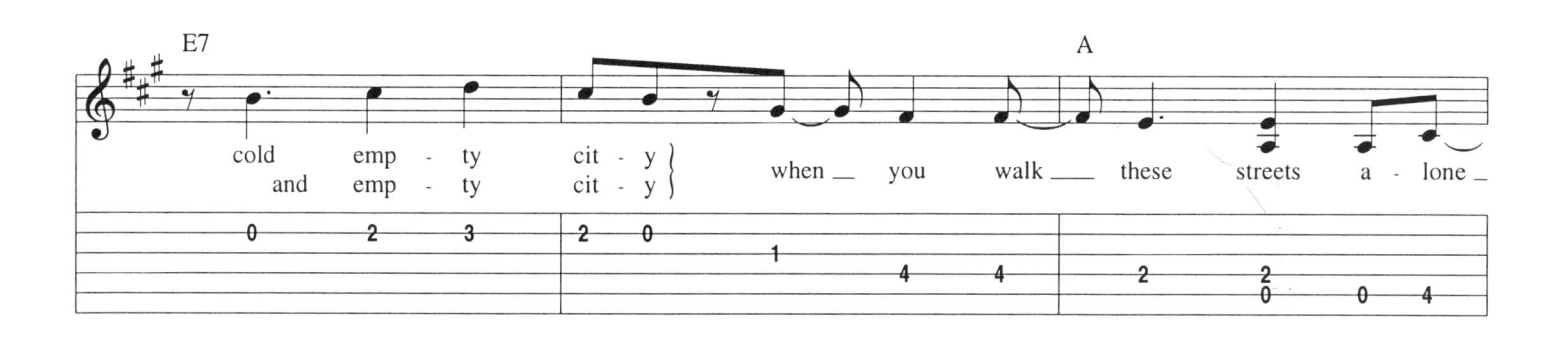

And it's a day-to-day surviv-al in a bat-tle zone, and a, a blue jungle with you gone.

Chorus

It's a blue
And it's a blue jungle with you gone.

And it's a
It's a cold cold empty city
and empty city
when you walk these streets a-lone

Bm7
like a wild pan - ther scream - in' when you hear a whis-tle moan,
D E7 A
and a
It's a
blue jun - gle with you gone.
1. 2.
A7
Outro
D
And it's a blue
E7 A
jun - gle with you gone.

Additional Lyrics

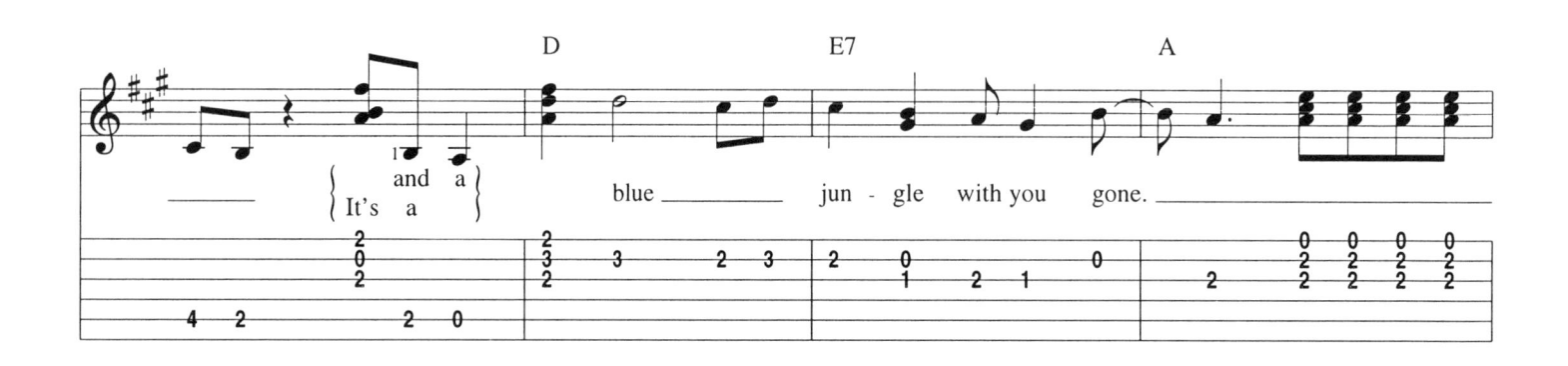

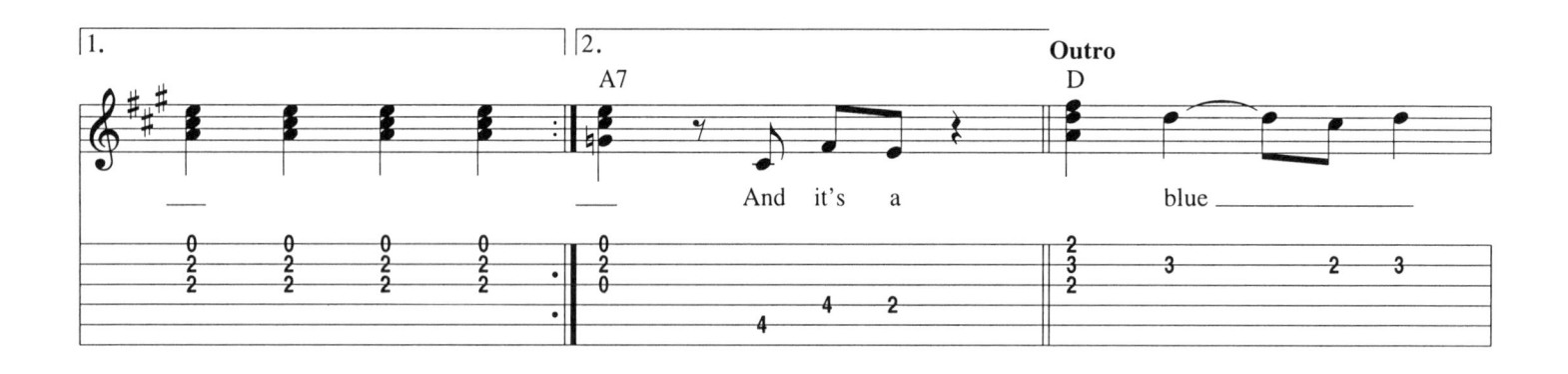

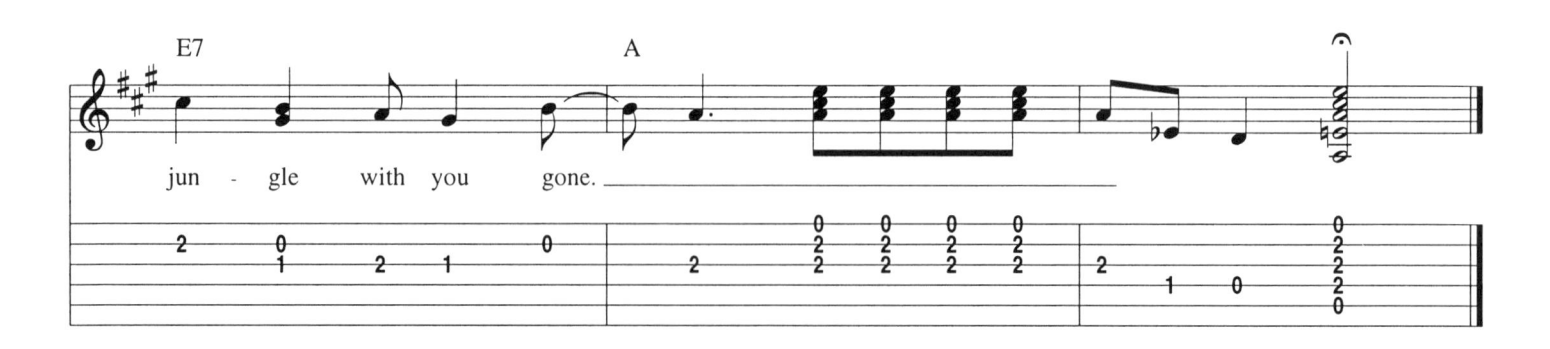

2. The weekend party's over and I'm sober once again,
   And it's hard to face the world without my friend.
   And it's dog eat dog existence just to make it on your own,
   And a, a blue jungle with you gone.

Carolyn

Words and Music by Tommy Collins

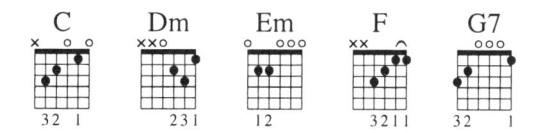

Chords: C, Dm, Em, F, G7

Strum Pattern: 2, 3
Pick Pattern: 3, 4

Intro
Ballad Tempo

Verse

Car-o-lyn, ___ let me tell you what I've heard 'bout a man ___ to-day. ___

He did-n't come home from work and he went a-way, ___

till he came ___ to a cit-y ___

Copyright © 1971 Sony/ATV Songs LLC
Copyright Renewed
All Rights Administered by Sony/ATV Music Publishing, 8 Music Square West, Nashville, TN 37203
International Copyright Secured All Rights Reserved

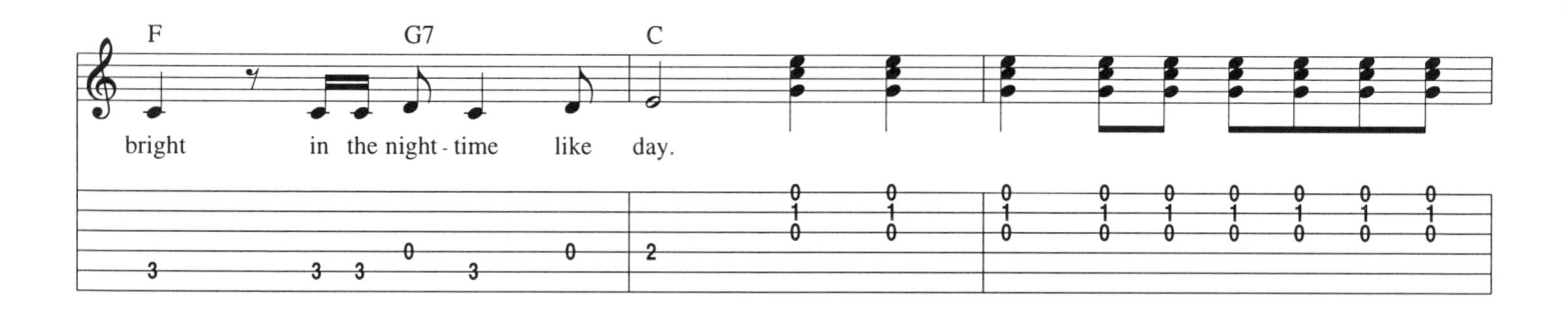

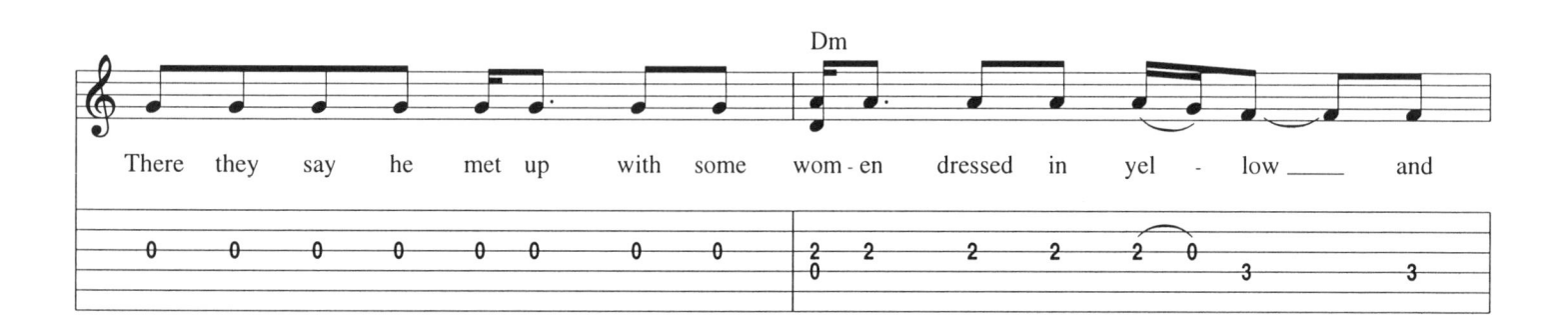

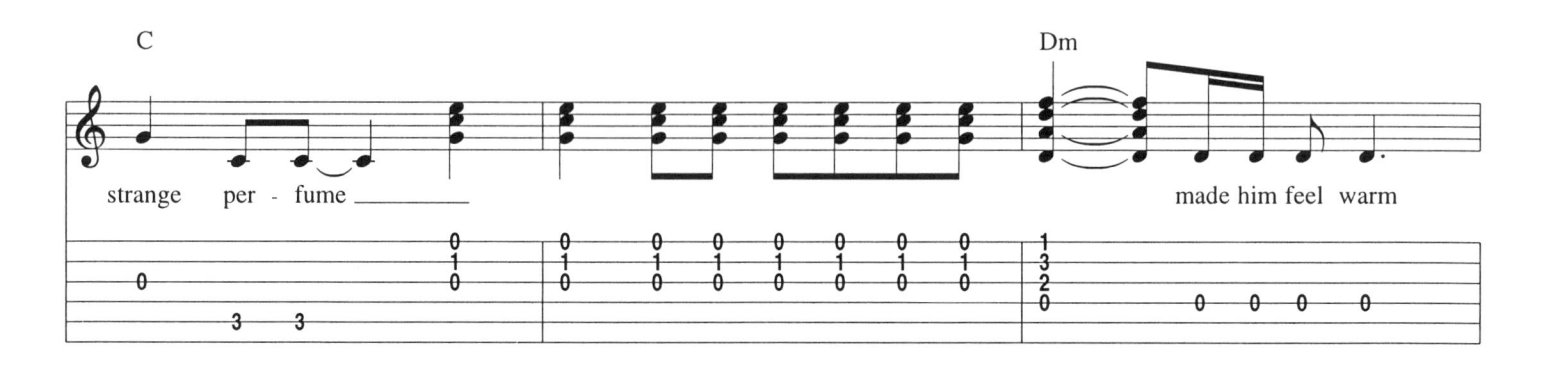

bright in the night-time like day. There they say he met up with some women dressed in yellow and scarlet, their warm lips like a honeycomb dripped with honey. And something about the smell of strange perfume made him feel warm

Chorus

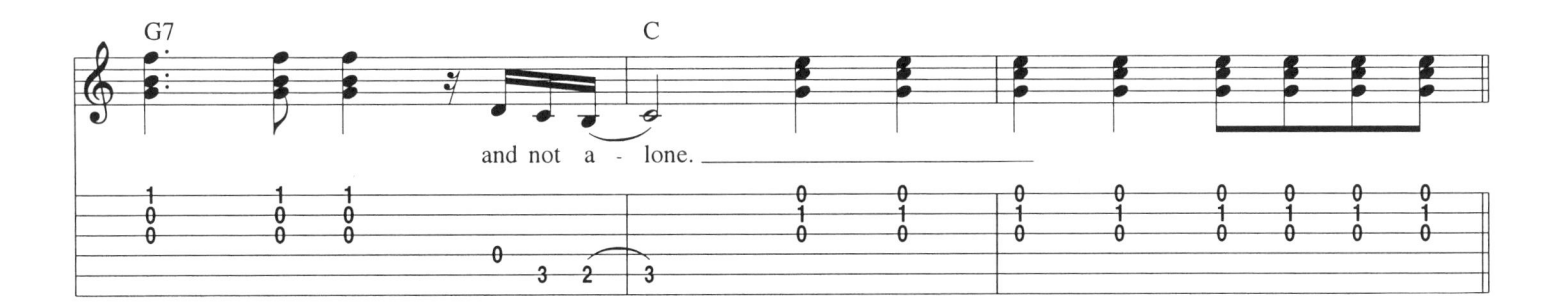

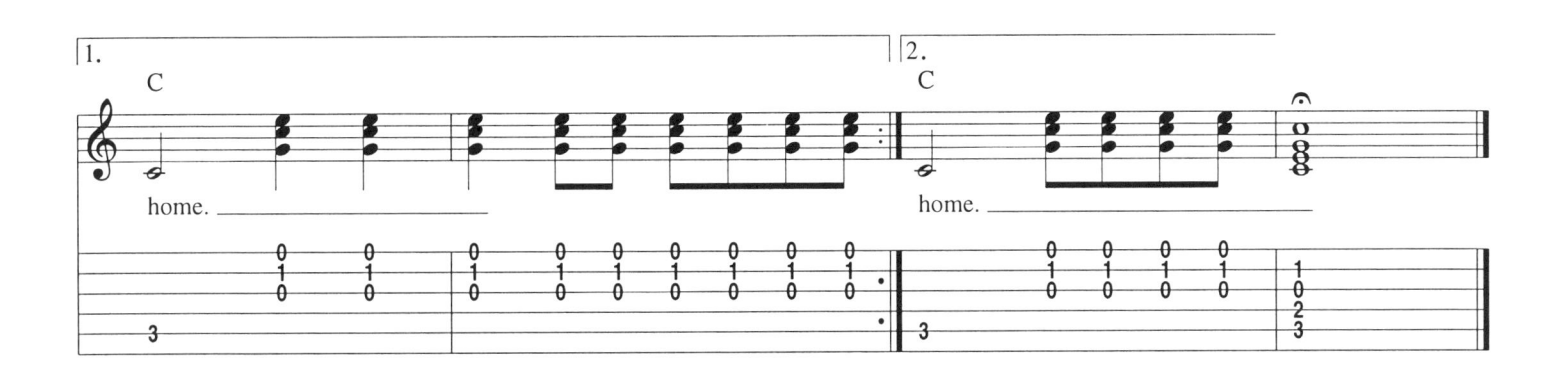

Yes, Car-o-lyn, a man will do that some-times on his own, some-times when he's lone-ly. And I be-lieve a man might do that some-times out of spite, but Car-o-lyn, a man will do that al-ways when he's treat-ed bad at home.

1. home.
2. home.

The Emptiest Arms in the World

Words and Music by Merle Haggard

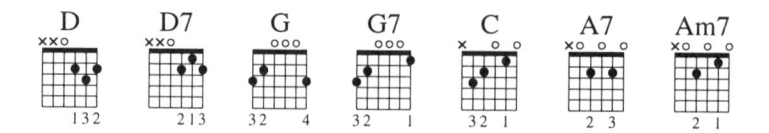

Strum Pattern: 2, 3
Pick Pattern: 3, 4

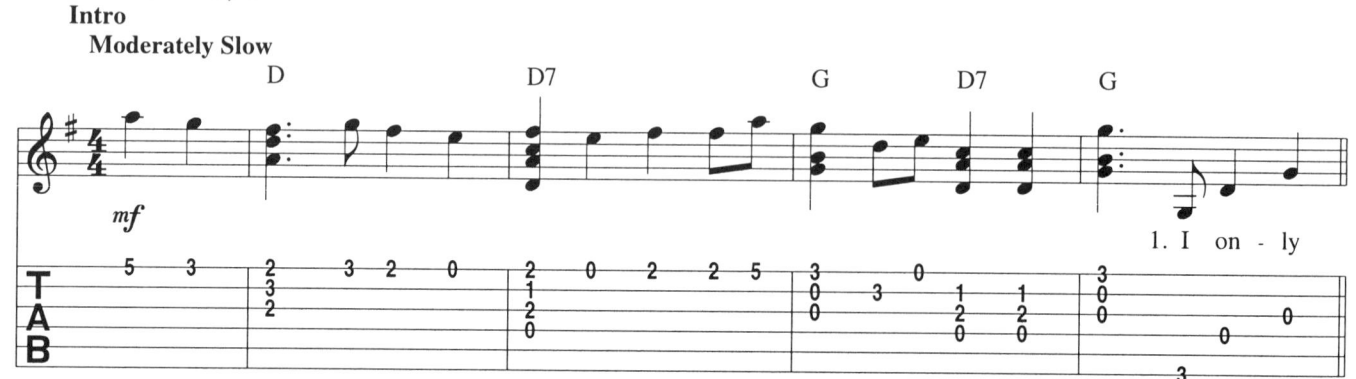

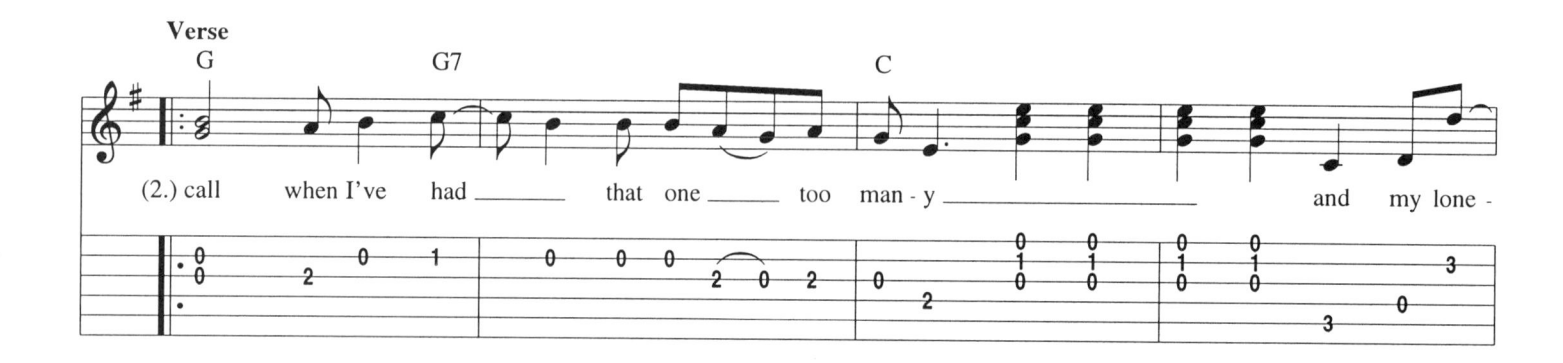

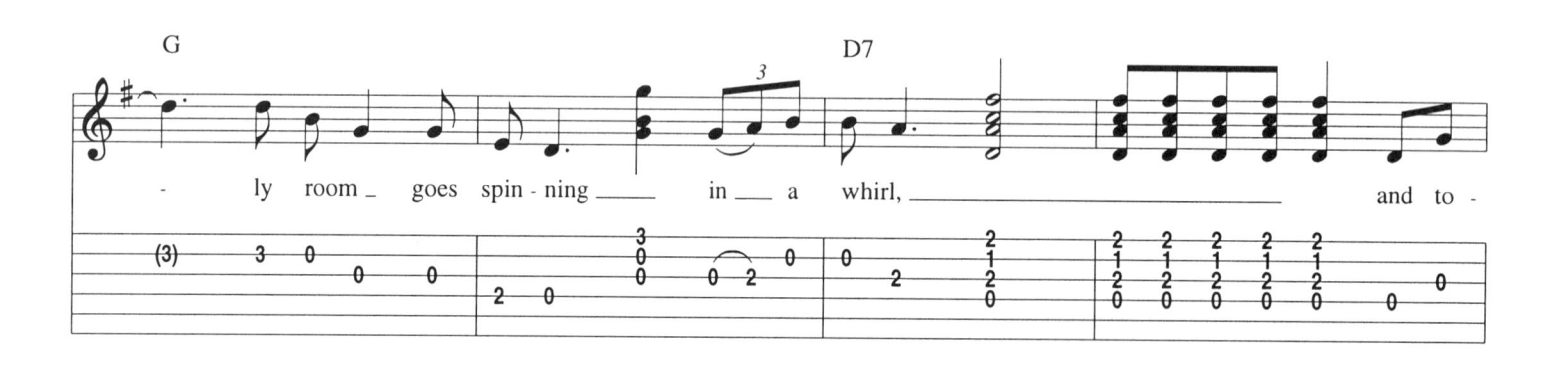

Intro
Moderately Slow

1. I only (2.) call when I've had that one too many and my lonely room goes spinning in a whirl, and tonight I couldn't even find my pillow. I've got the

Copyright © 1973 Sony/ATV Songs LLC
All Rights Administered by Sony/ATV Music Publishing, 8 Music Square West, Nashville, TN 37203
International Copyright Secured   All Rights Reserved

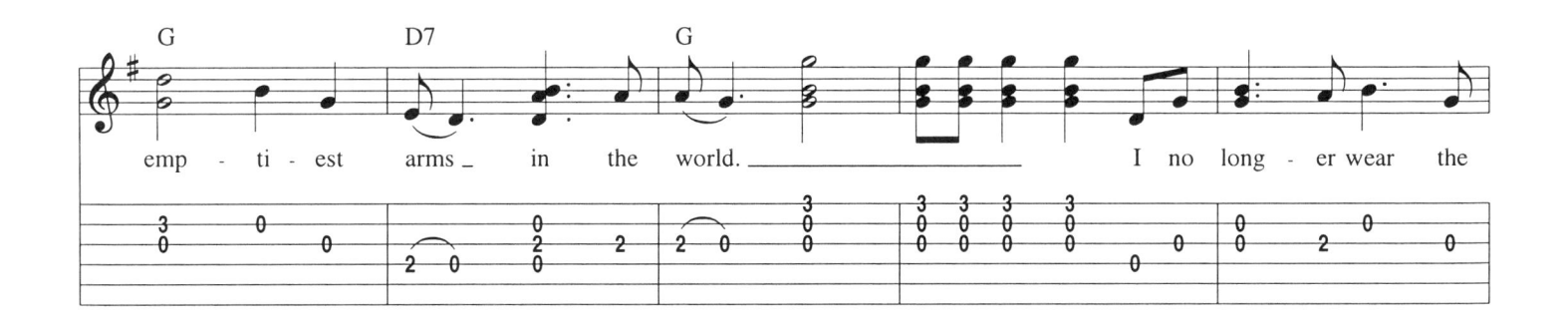

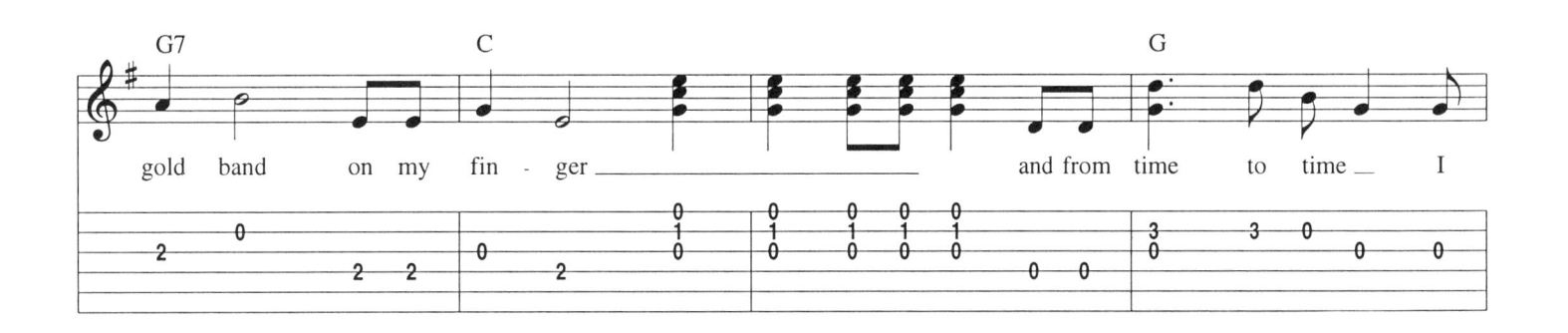

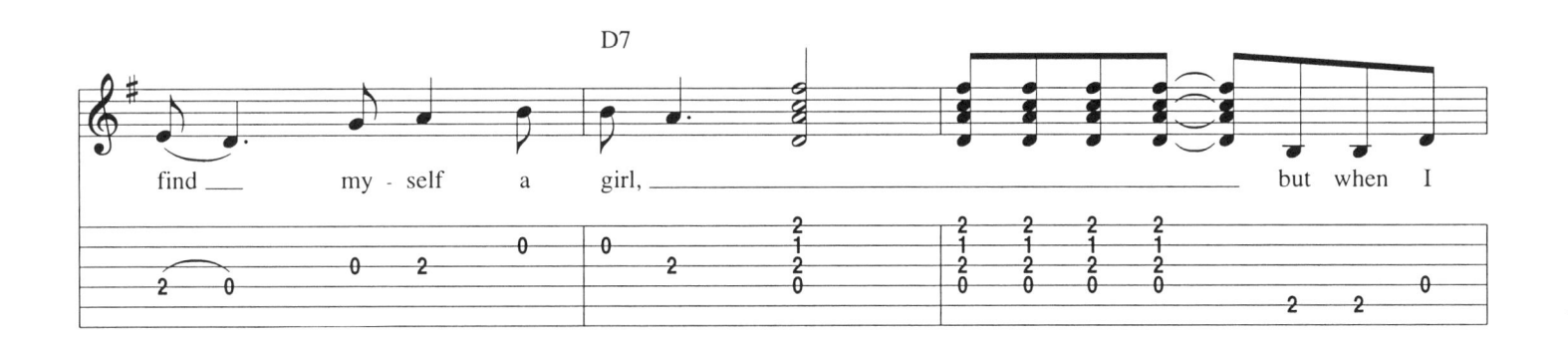

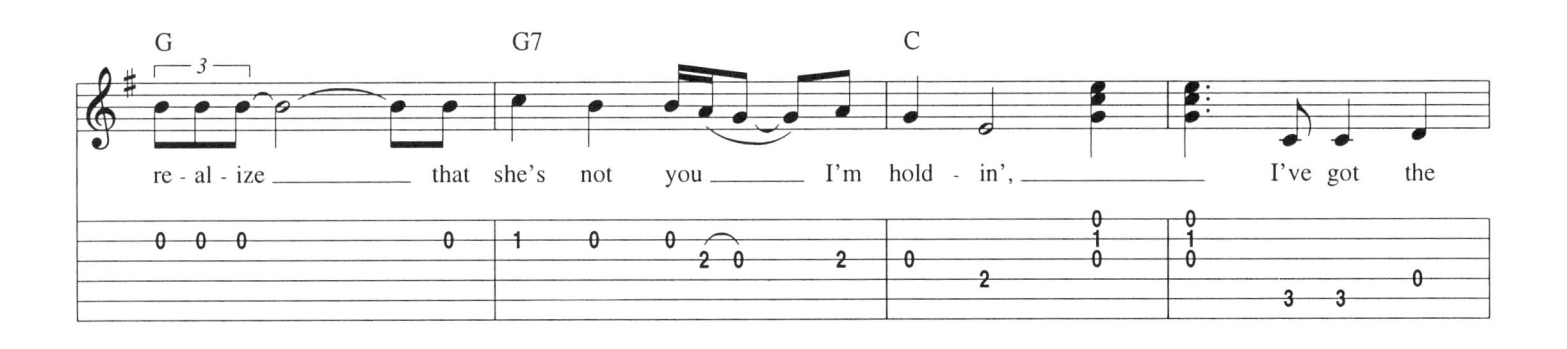

emp - ti - est arms in the world. I no long - er wear the gold band on my fin - ger and from time to time I find my - self a girl, but when I re - al - ize that she's not you I'm hold - in', I've got the emp - ti - est arms in the world. My emp - ty

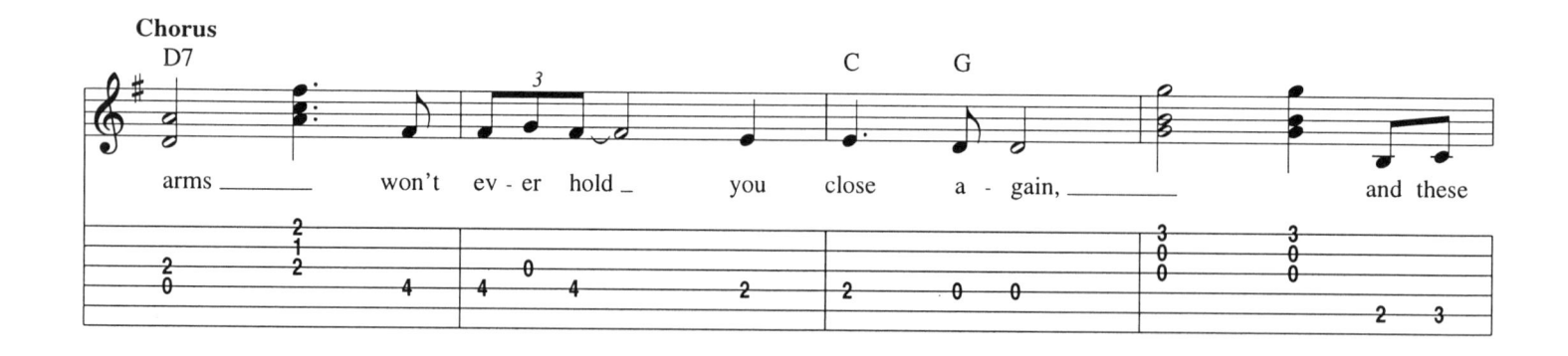

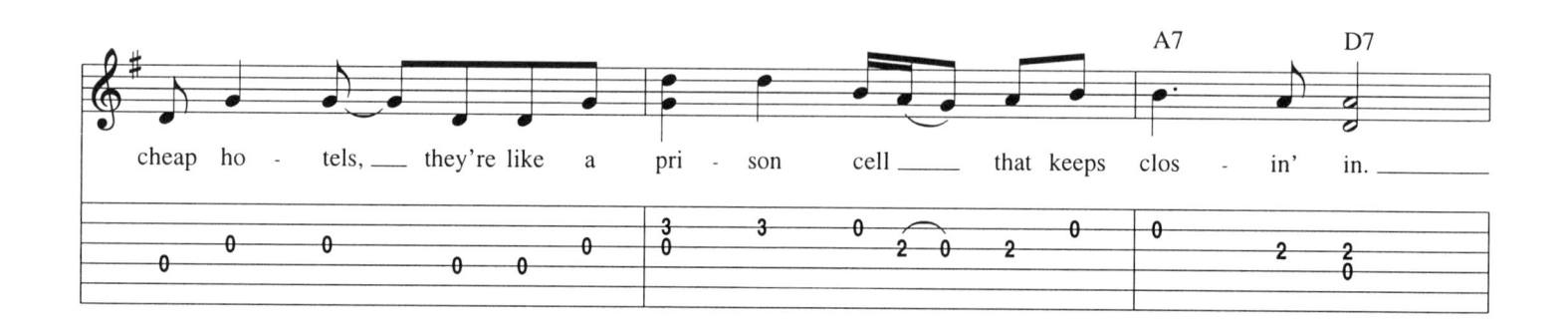

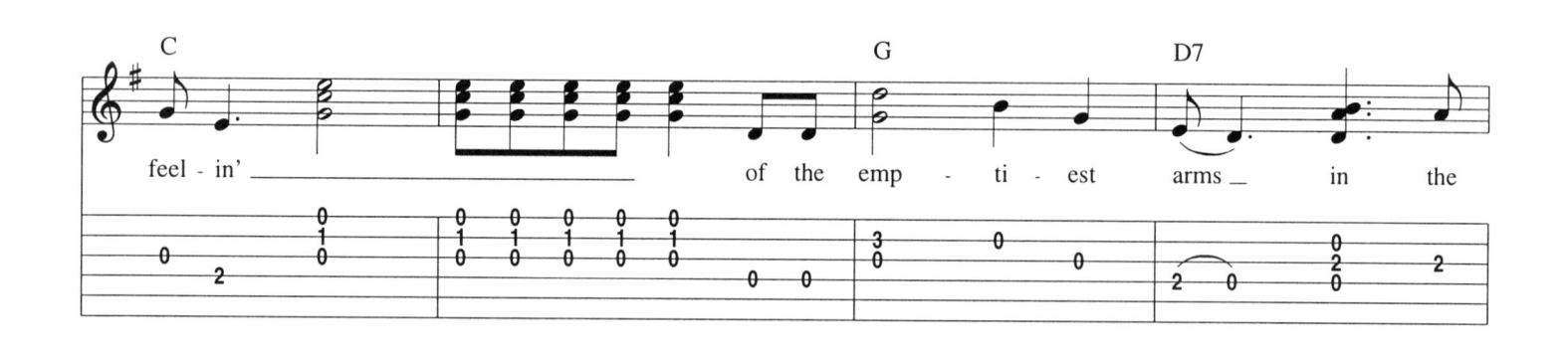

Chorus

arms _____ won't ev-er hold ___ you close a-gain, _____ and these cheap ho-tels, ___ they're like a pri-son cell ____ that keeps clos-in' in. _____

{Now / And} you a-lone _____ can fill this {lone-ly / emp-ty} feel-in' _____ of the emp-ti-est arms ___ in the world. _____ 2. I on-ly world. _____

I Had a Beautiful Time

Words and Music by Merle Haggard

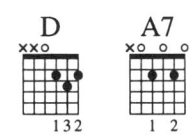

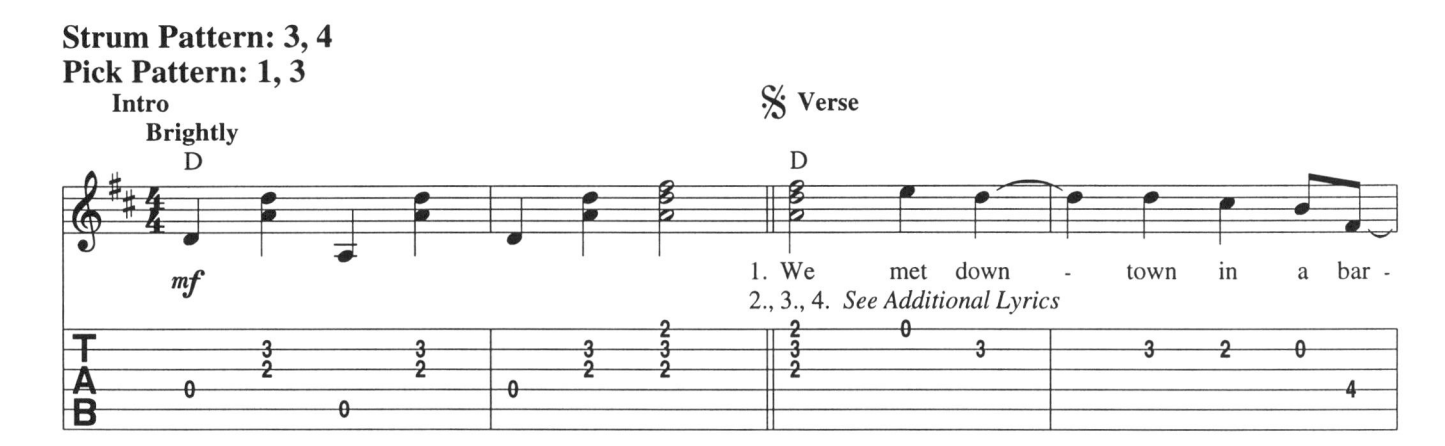

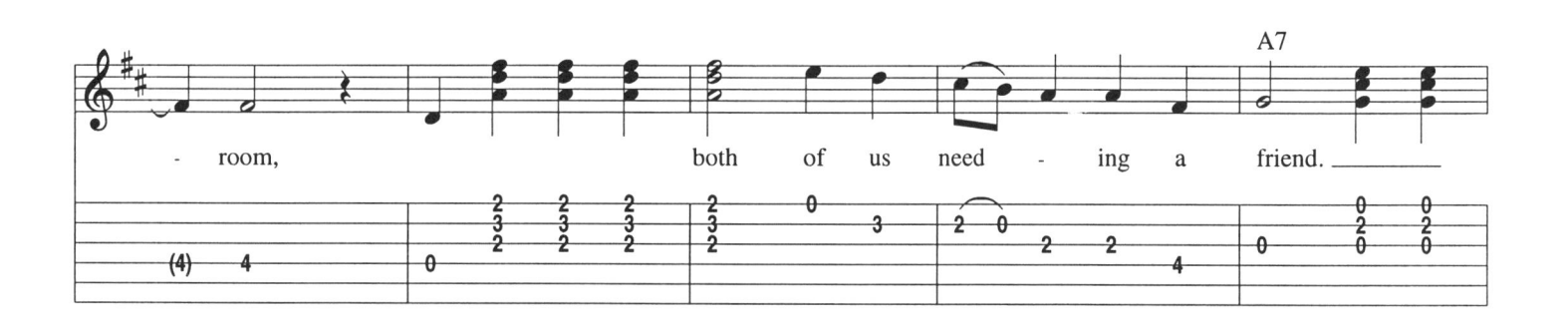

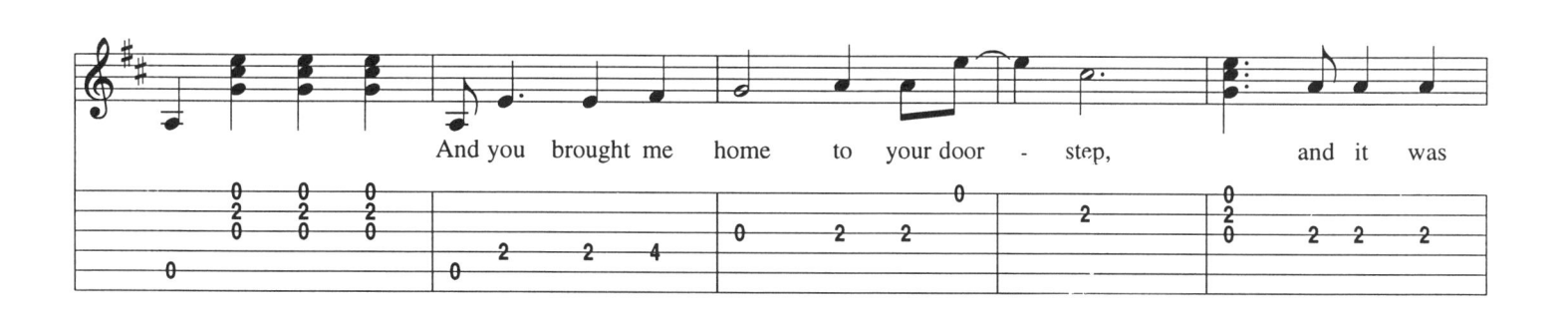

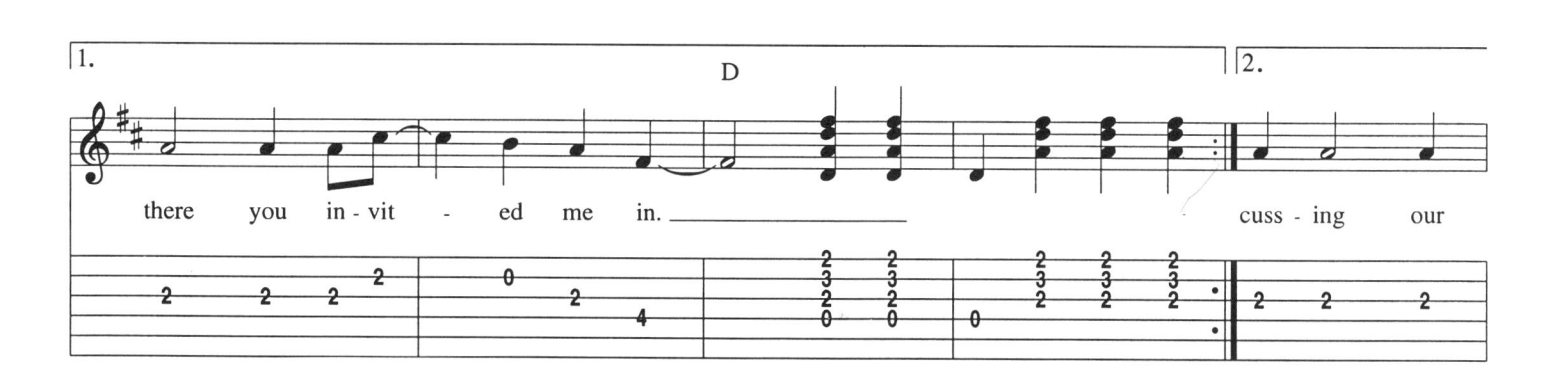

Strum Pattern: 3, 4
Pick Pattern: 1, 3

Intro
Brightly

1. We met downtown in a barroom, both of us needing a friend. And you brought me home to your doorstep, and it was there you invited me in.

2., 3., 4. *See Additional Lyrics*

2. cuss-ing our

Copyright © 1977 Sony/ATV Songs LLC
All Rights Administered by Sony/ATV Music Publishing, 8 Music Square West, Nashville, TN 37203
International Copyright Secured   All Rights Reserved

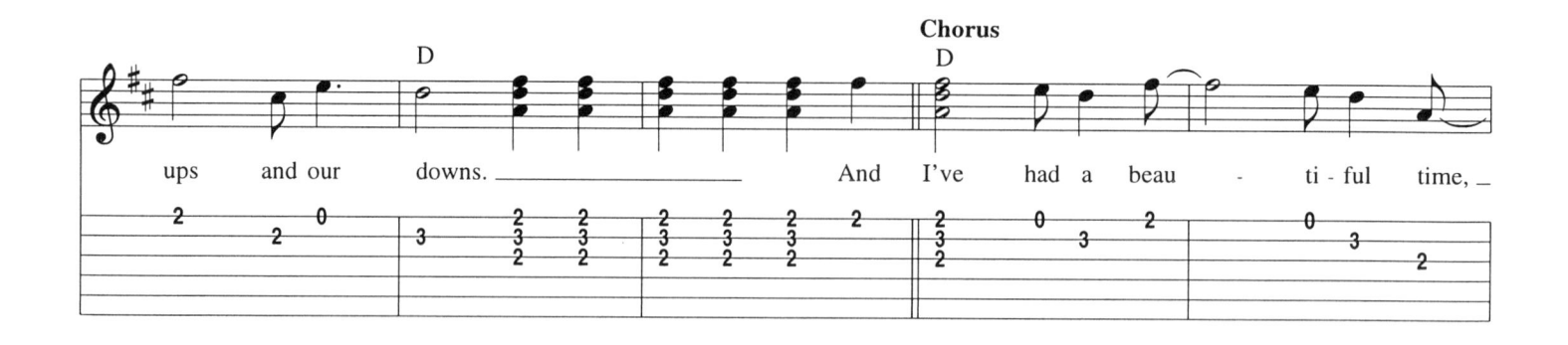

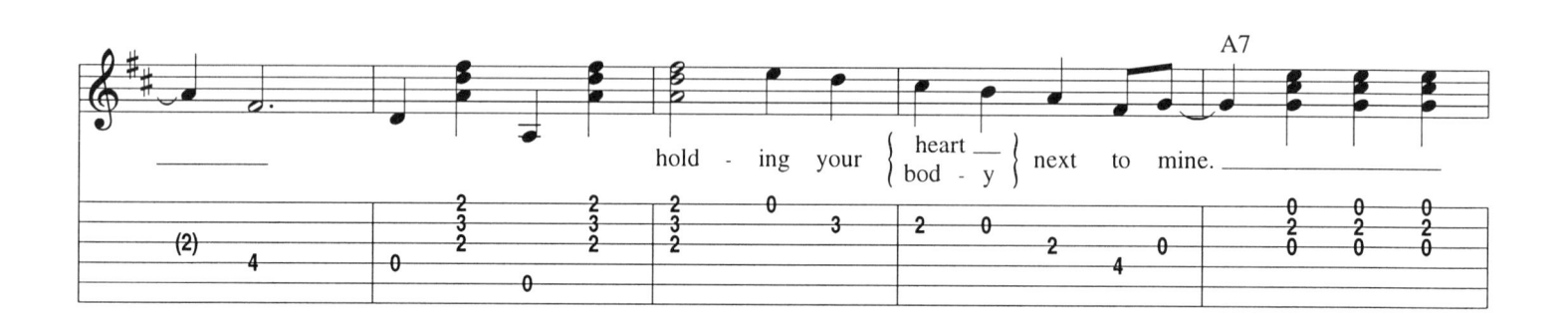

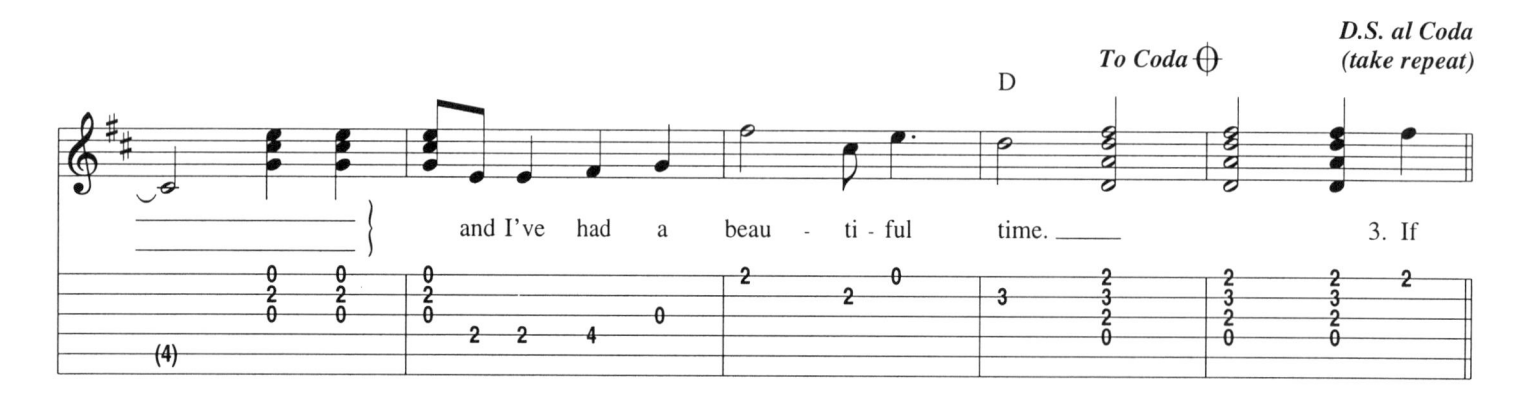

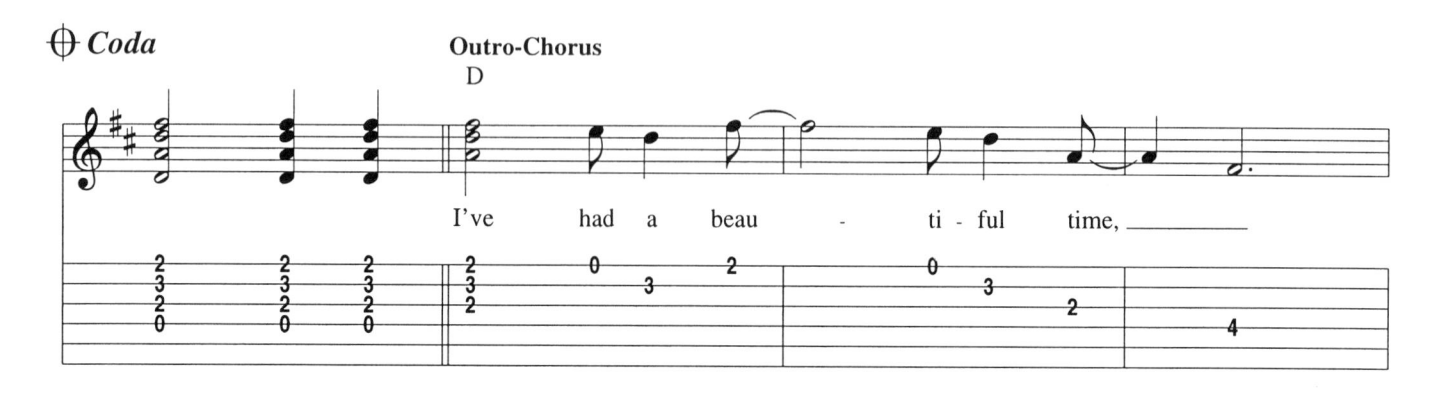

ups and our downs. And I've had a beau-ti-ful time,

hold-ing your { heart / bod-y } next to mine.

{ I poured out my feel-ings, while you poured the wine,
You poured out your feel-ings, and I poured the wine, }

and I've had a beau-ti-ful time. 3. If

Coda

Outro-Chorus

I've had a beau-ti-ful time,

holding your heart next to mine.

We poured out our feelings and then we poured the wine,
You poured out your feelings while we poured the wine,

and I've had a beautiful time.

Additional Lyrics

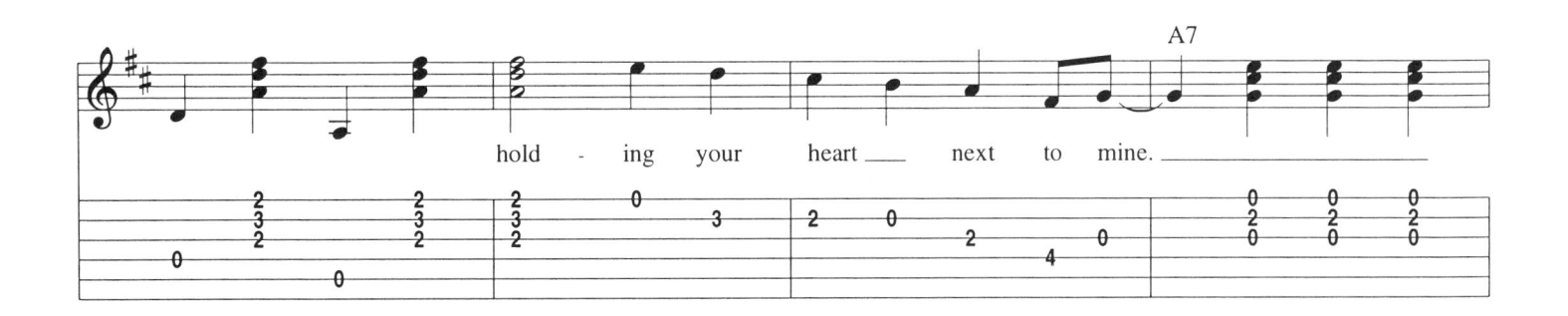

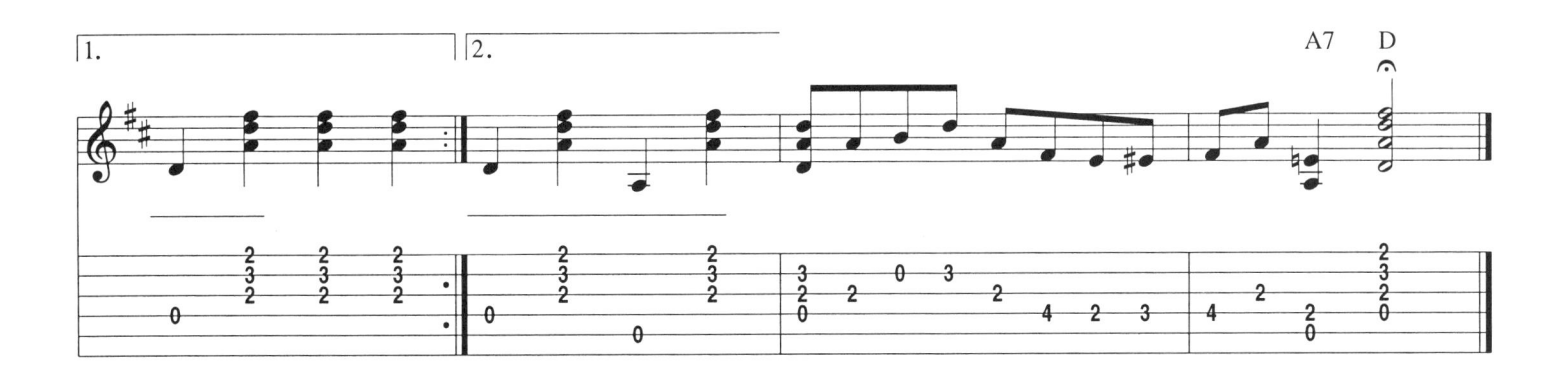

2. We spent the wee hours dancing
   To your favorite home stereo sounds.
   We talked about what we'd been needing,
   Discussing our ups and our downs.

3. If I seem a wee bit uneasy,
   Then you really sized me up right.
   There's somebody home still up waiting;
   She's probably been up waiting all night.

4. And I can't say I found any answers,
   But you listened while I rattled on.
   And you've been a beautiful lady;
   And you kept me from being alone.

From Graceland to the Promised Land

Words and Music by Merle Haggard

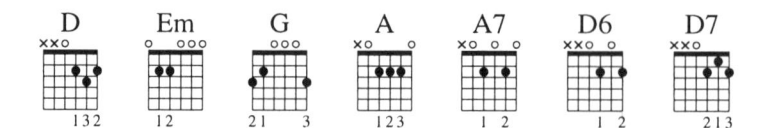

Strum Pattern: 3, 4
Pick Pattern: 1, 3

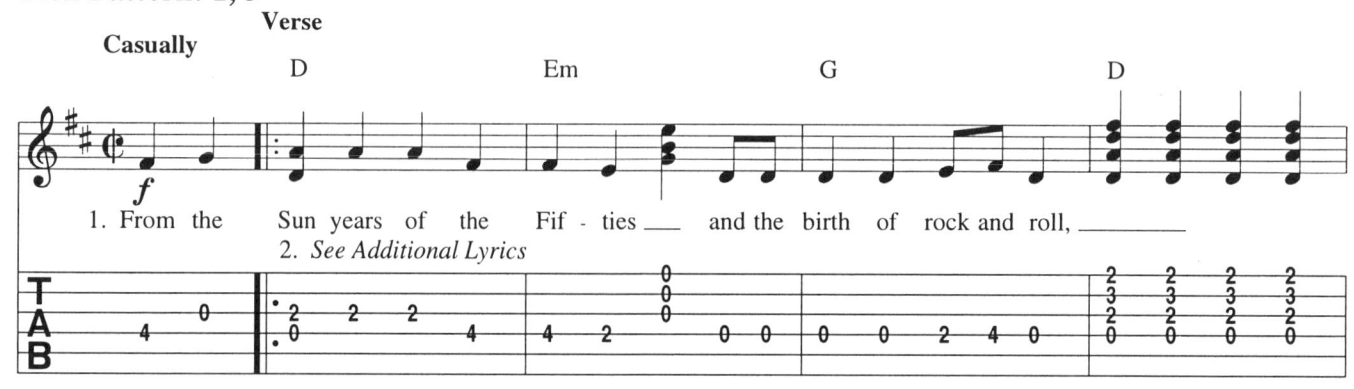

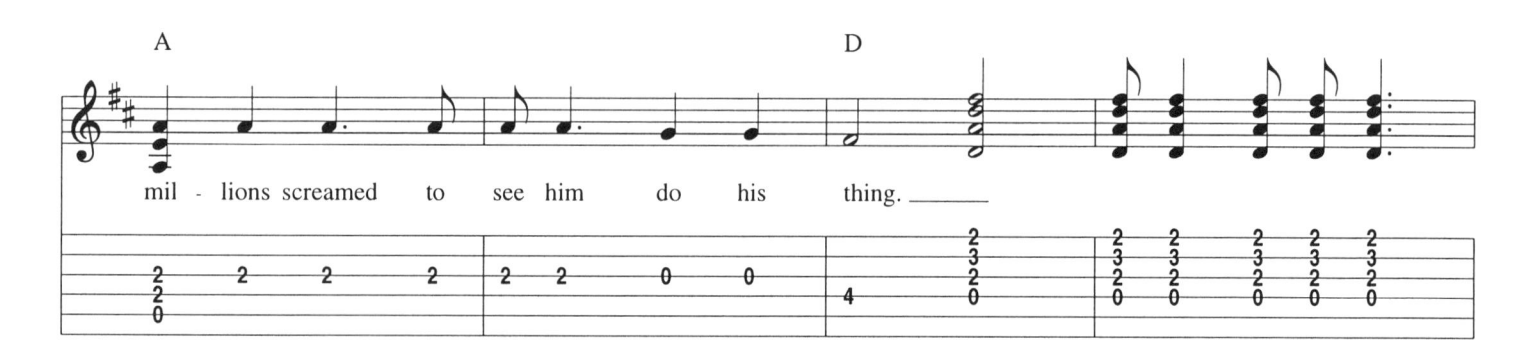

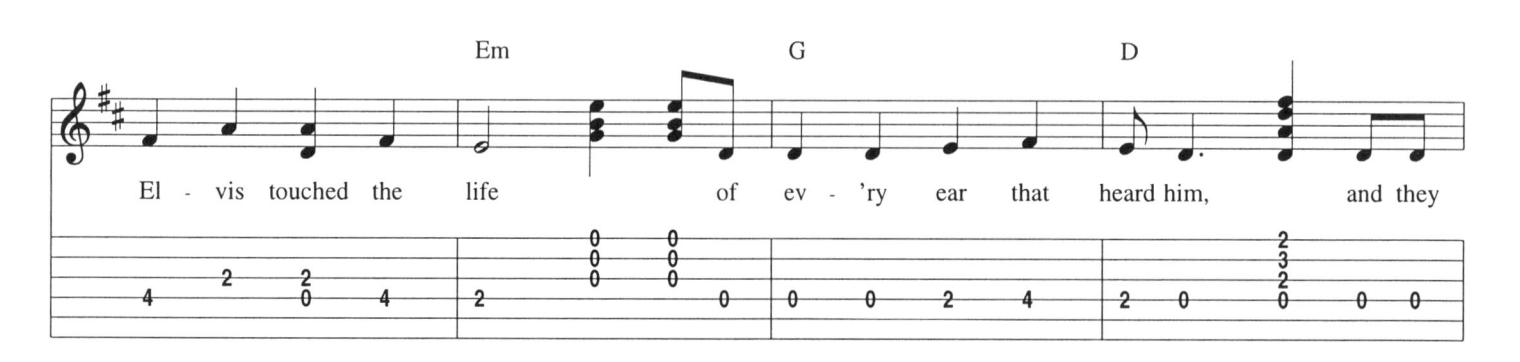

Casually

Verse

1. From the Sun years of the Fif-ties and the birth of rock and roll, mil-lions screamed to see him do his thing. El-vis touched the life of ev-'ry ear that heard him, and they could-n't help but lis-ten when he sang. It's a

2. *See Additional Lyrics*

Chorus

long way from Memphis to that mansion in the sky, but he kept his faith in Jesus all along. It's a long way from Graceland across Jordan to the Promised Land, but Jesus fin-'ly came to lead him home.

2. From the home.

Additional Lyrics

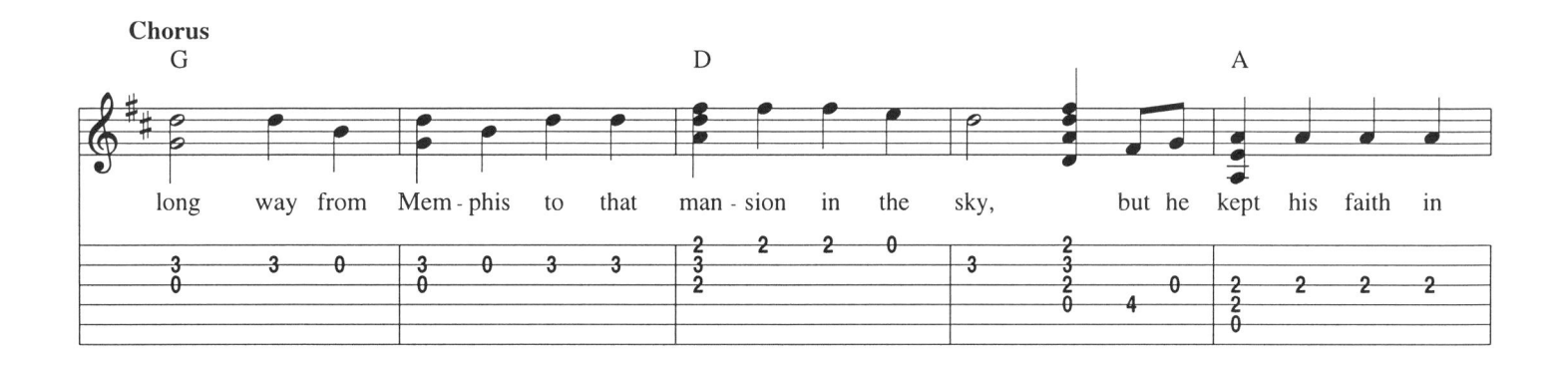

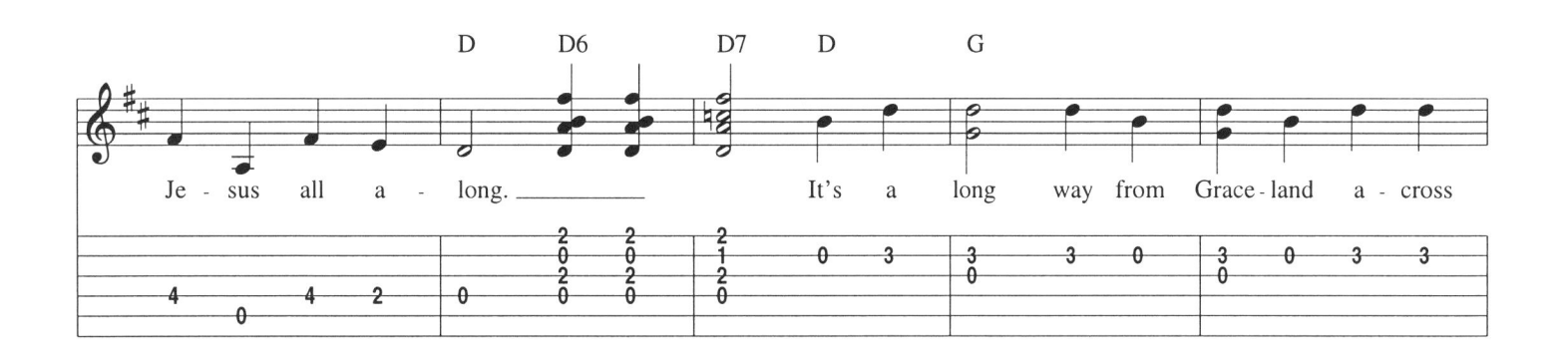

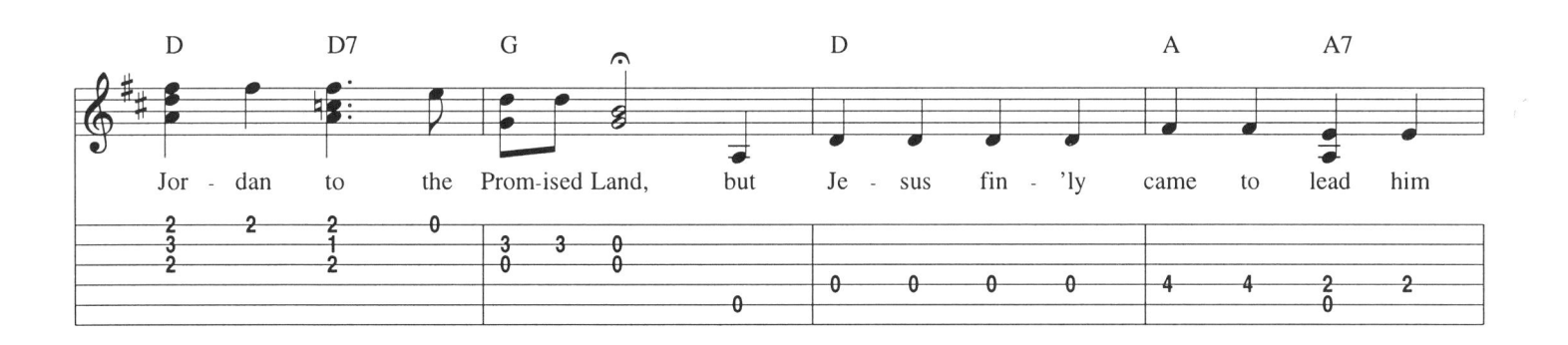

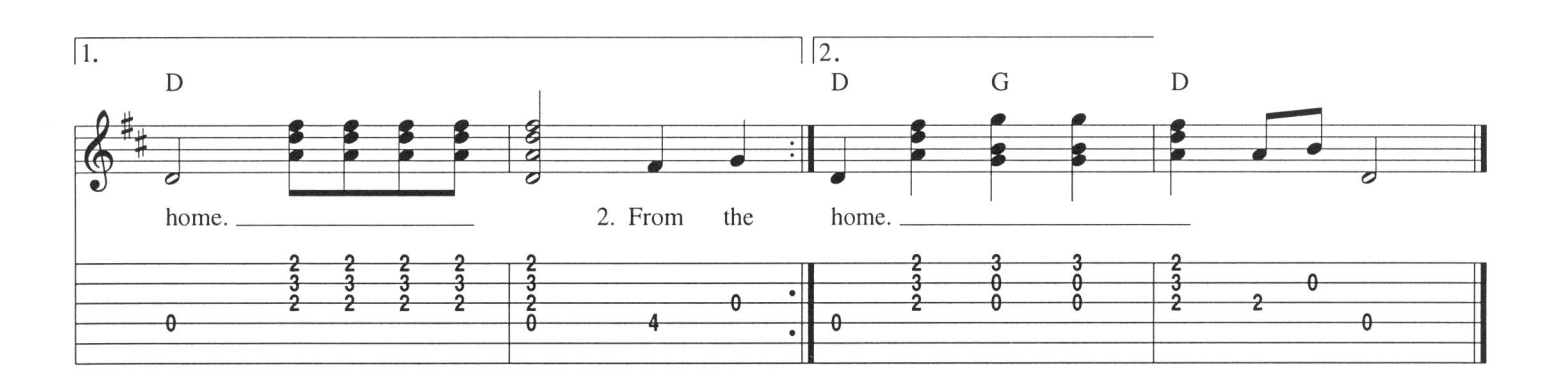

2. From the days of "Love Me Tender"
   To his Mama's last farewell,
   Some say he knew how long he had to stay.
   His life was two days longer
   Than the one who gave him life,
   And he almost knew the number of the days.

I Started Loving You Again

Words and Music by Merle Haggard

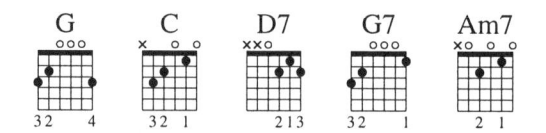

G C D7 G7 Am7

Strum Pattern: 3, 4
Pick Pattern: 1, 3

Intro
Moderately

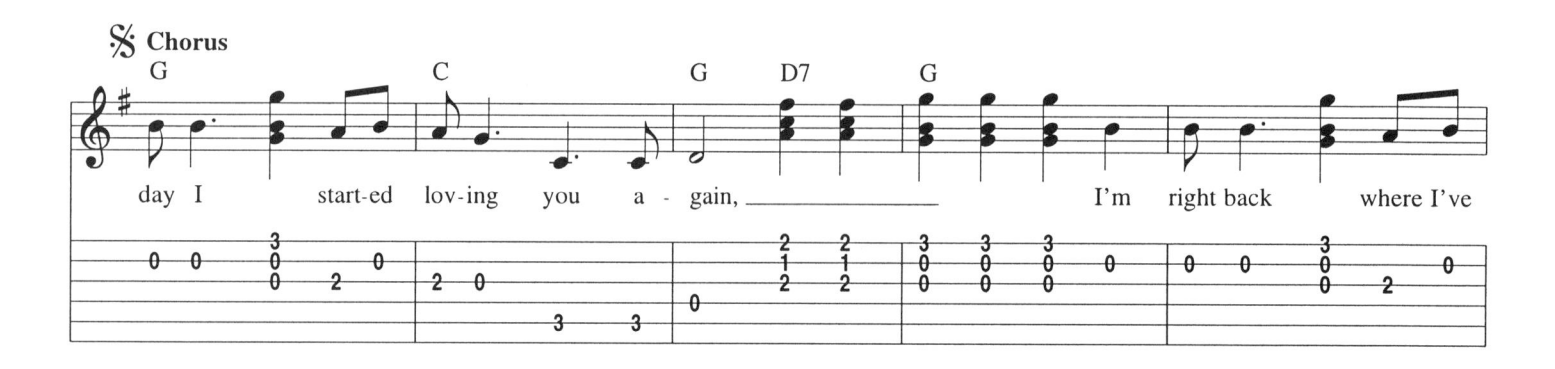

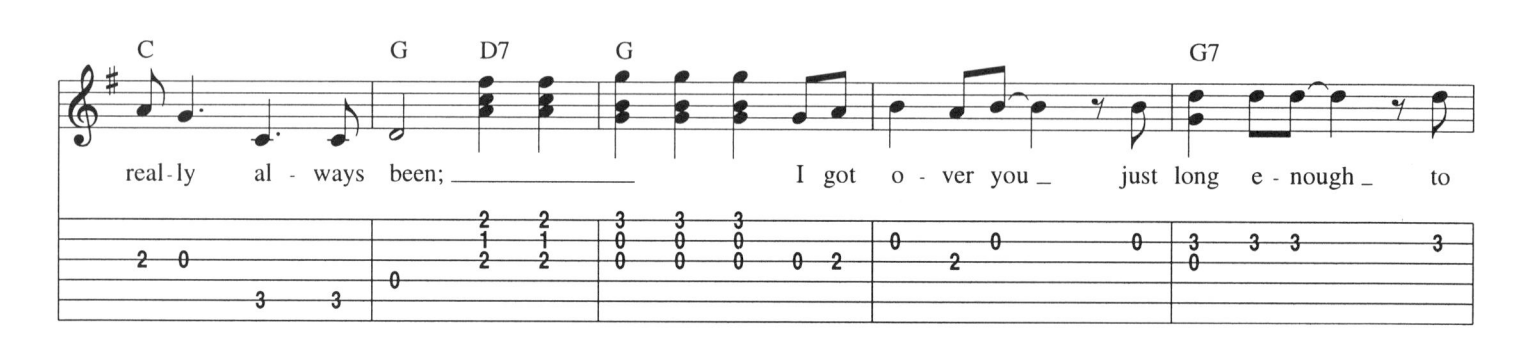

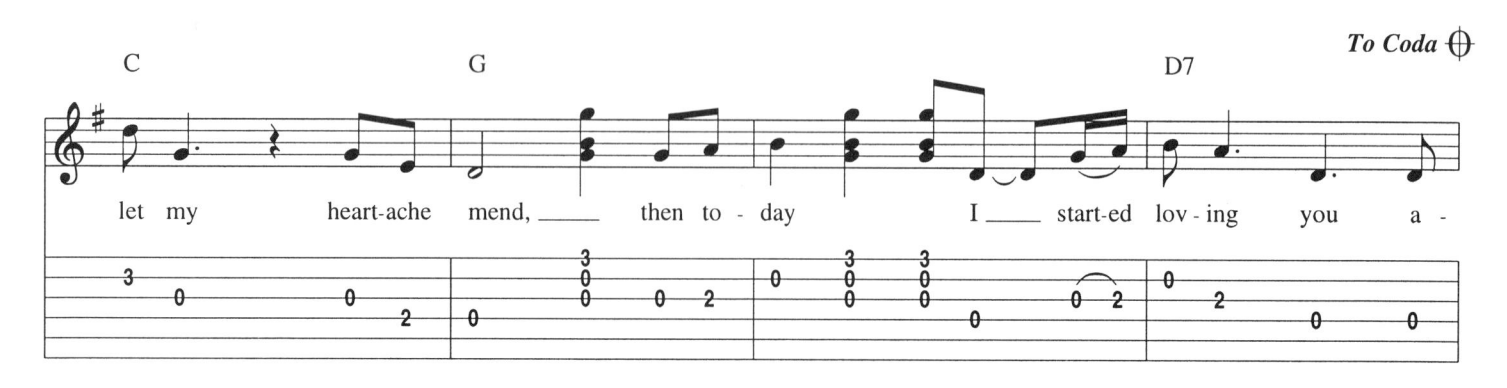

To-

Chorus

day I start-ed lov-ing you a-gain, ___ I'm right back where I've

real-ly al-ways been; ___ I got o-ver you __ just long e-nough __ to

To Coda

let my heart-ache mend, ___ then to-day I __ start-ed lov-ing you a-

Verse
G G C G
gain. What a fool I was to think I could get by
C D7
with on-ly these few mil-lion tears I've cried. I
G C G
should have known the worst was yet to come and that
D.S. al Coda
D7 G
cry-ing time for me had just be-gun. 'Cause to-
Coda
G C G Am7 G
gain.

I Think I'll Just Stay Here and Drink

Words and Music by Merle Haggard

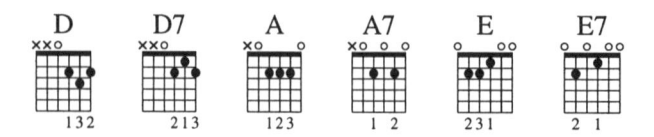

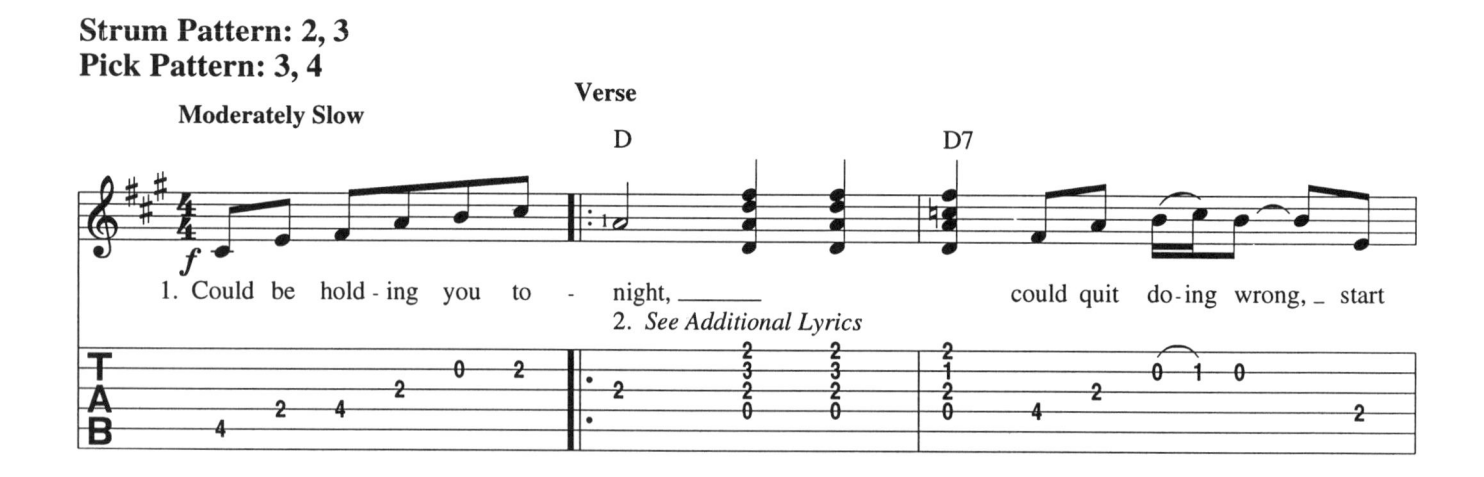

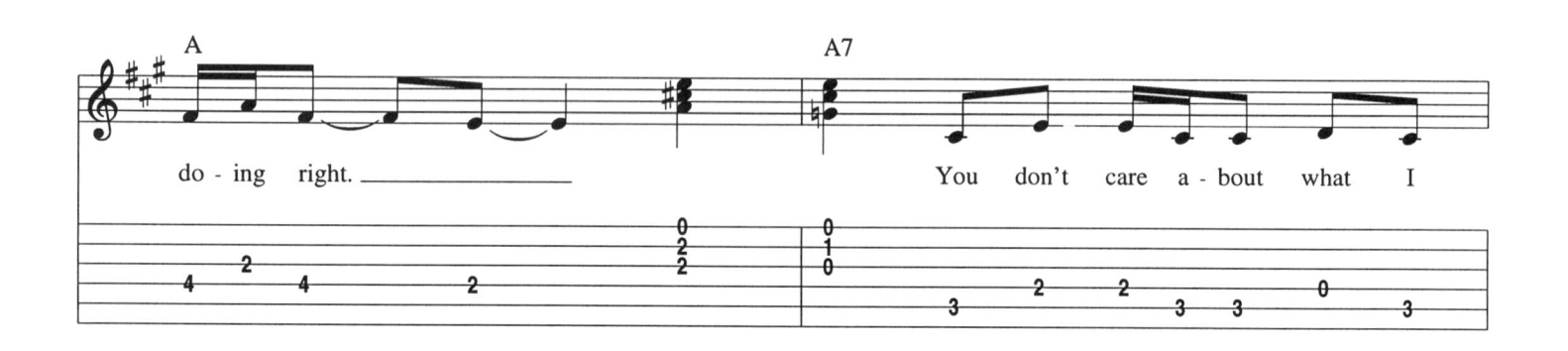

Chords: D, D7, A, A7, E, E7

Strum Pattern: 2, 3
Pick Pattern: 3, 4

Moderately Slow

1. Could be holding you tonight, could quit doing wrong, start doing right.
2. *See Additional Lyrics*

You don't care about what I think... think I'll just stay here and drink.

Additional Lyrics

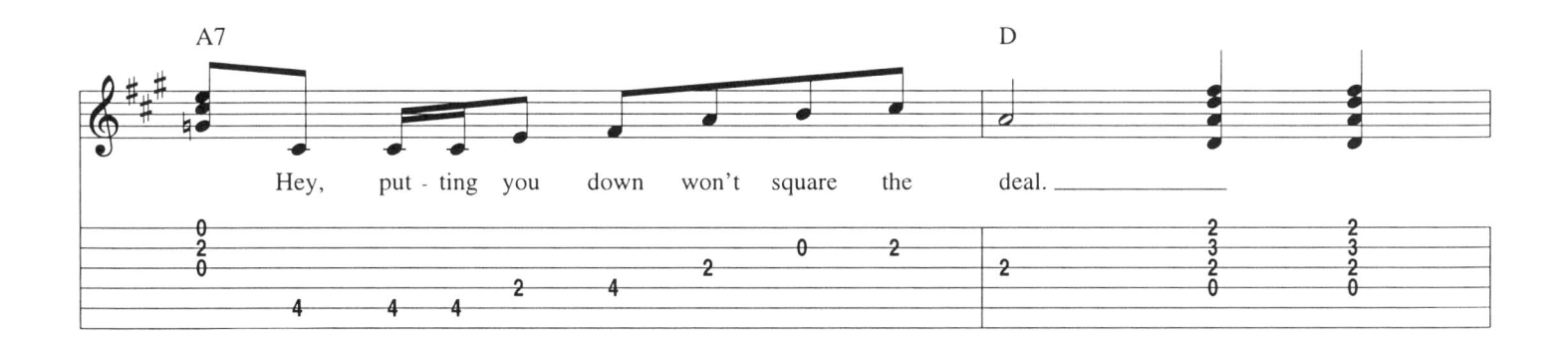

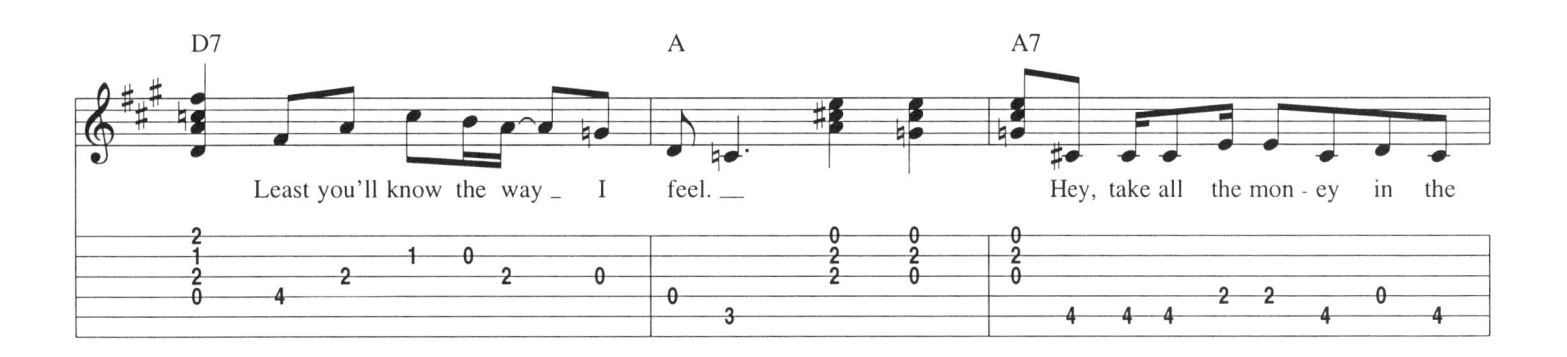

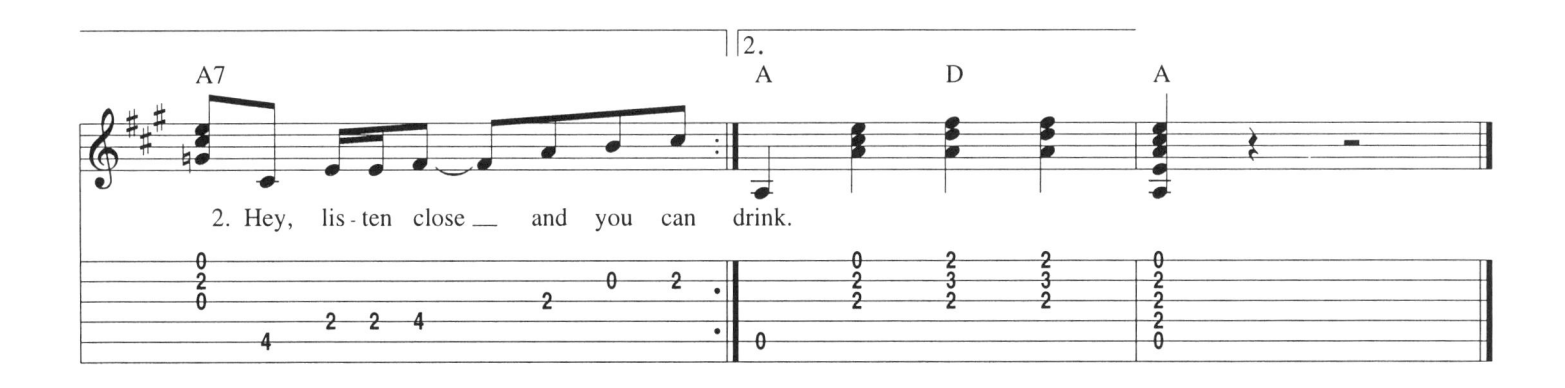

2. Hey, listen close and you can hear
   That loud jukebox playin' in my ear.
   Ain't no woman gon' change the way I think...
   Think I'll just stay here and drink.
   Hey, hurting me now don't mean a thing
   Since love ain't here. Don't feel the pain.
   My mind ain't nothing but a total blank...
   Think I'll just stay here and drink.

If We Make It Through December

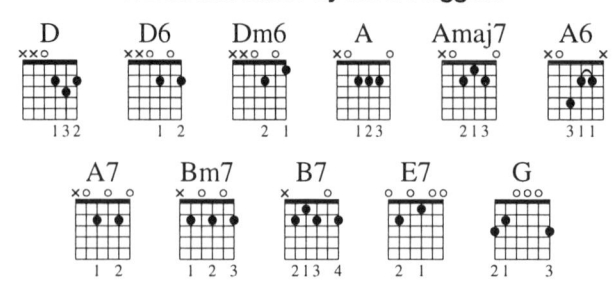

Words and Music by Merle Haggard

Chords: D, D6, Dm6, A, Amaj7, A6, A7, Bm7, B7, E7, G

Strum Pattern: 2, 4
Pick Pattern: 3, 4

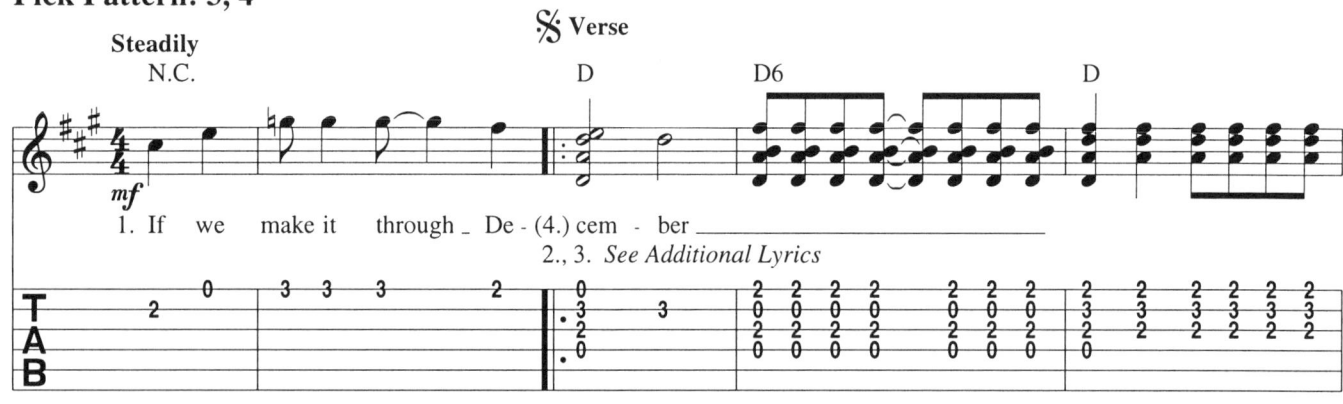

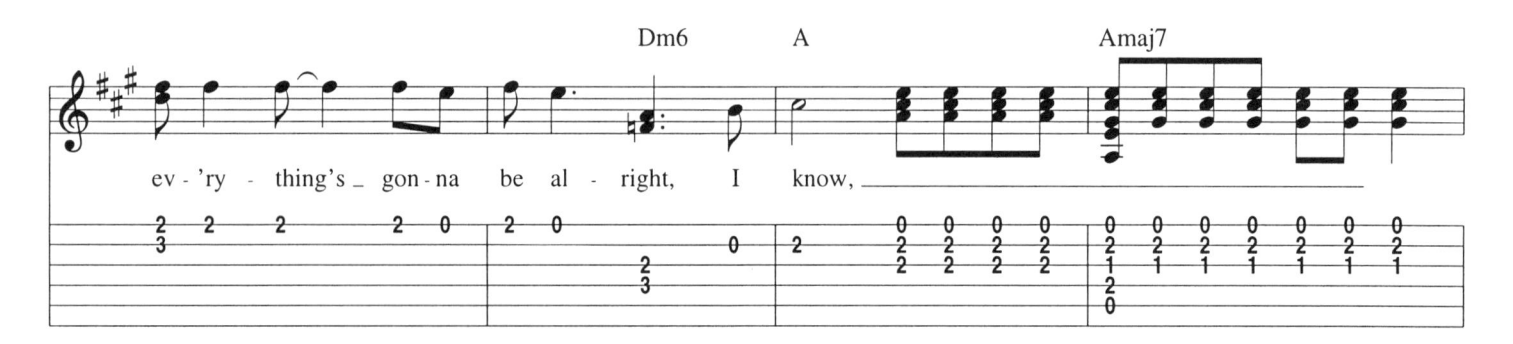

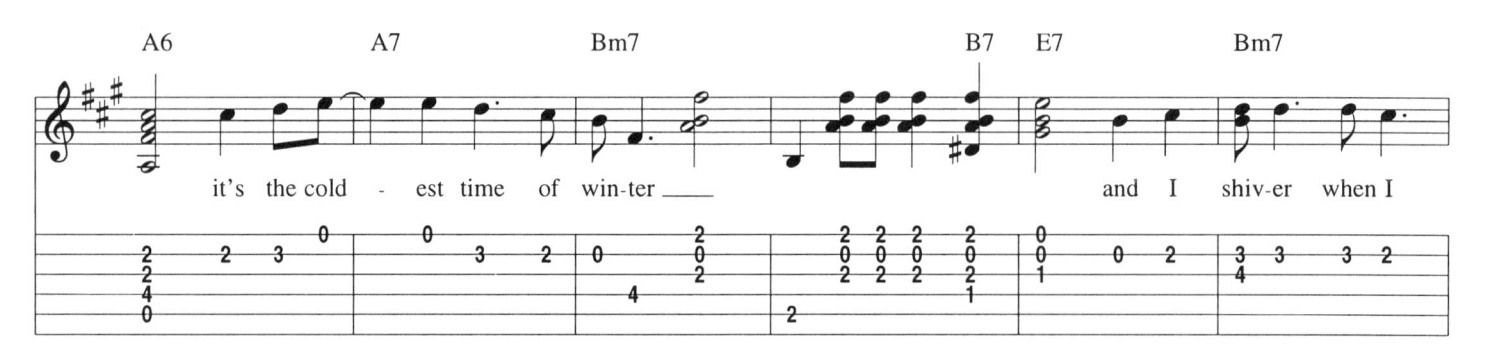

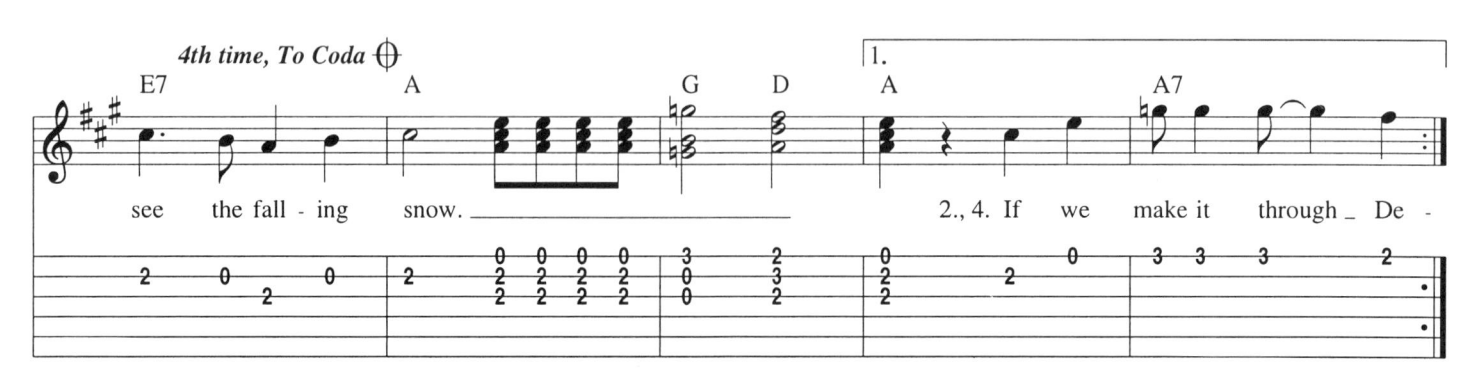

Steadily

1. If we make it through De-(4.)cem-ber
2., 3. *See Additional Lyrics*

ev'ry-thing's gon-na be al-right, I know,

it's the cold-est time of win-ter and I shiv-er when I

4th time, To Coda ⊕

see the fall-ing snow. 2., 4. If we make it through De-

Copyright © 1973 Sony/ATV Songs LLC
All Rights Administered by Sony/ATV Music Publishing, 8 Music Square West, Nashville, TN 37203
International Copyright Secured All Rights Reserved

Additional Lyrics

2. If we make it through December,
   Got plans to be in a warmer town come summertime,
   Maybe even California.
   If we make it through December, we'll be fine.

3. I don't mean to hate December,
   It's meant to be the happy time of year.
   And my little girl don't understand
   Why Daddy can't afford no Christmas here.

It's Been a Great Afternoon

Words and Music by Merle Haggard

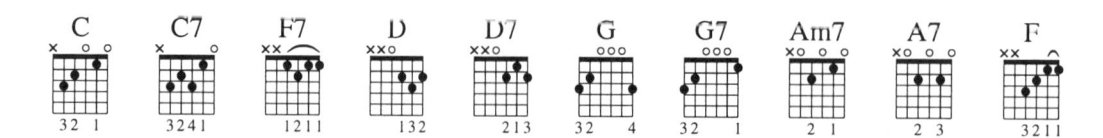

Strum Pattern: 3, 4
Pick Pattern: 1, 3

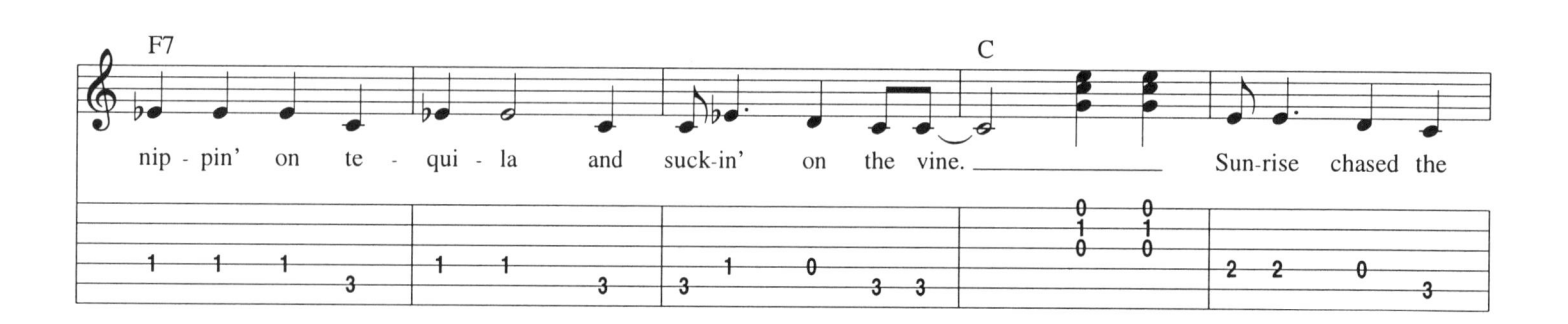

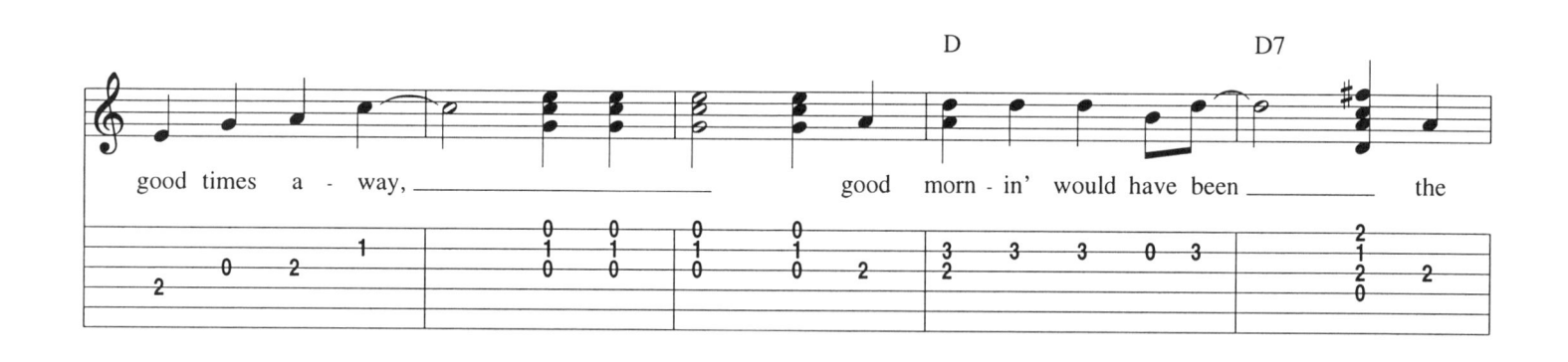

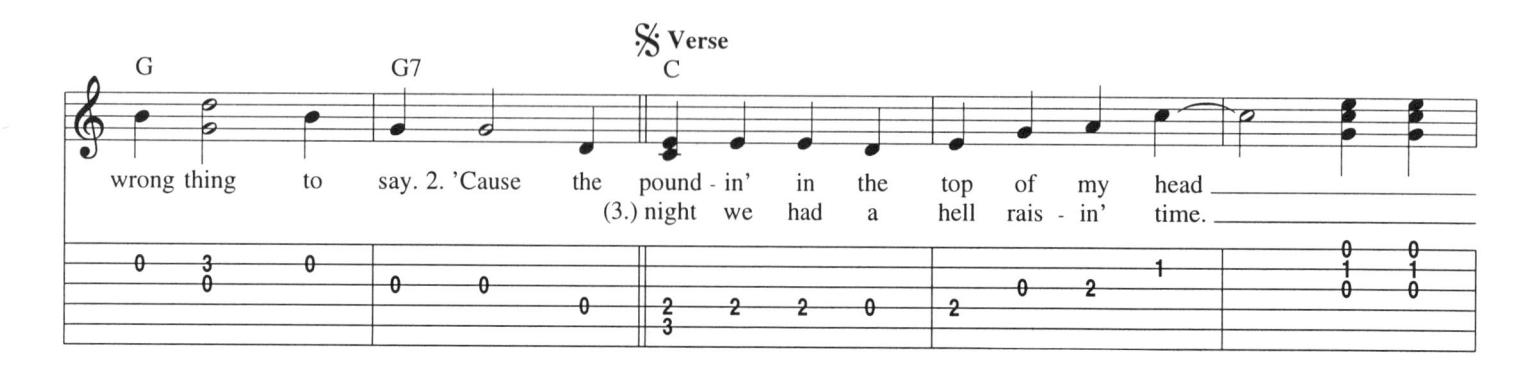

Verse
Bright Country

1. Last night we had a hell-rais-in' time, nip-pin' on te-qui-la and suck-in' on the vine. Sun-rise chased the good times a-way, good morn-in' would have been the wrong thing to say.

2. 'Cause the pound-in' in the top of my head

(3.) night we had a hell rais-in' time.

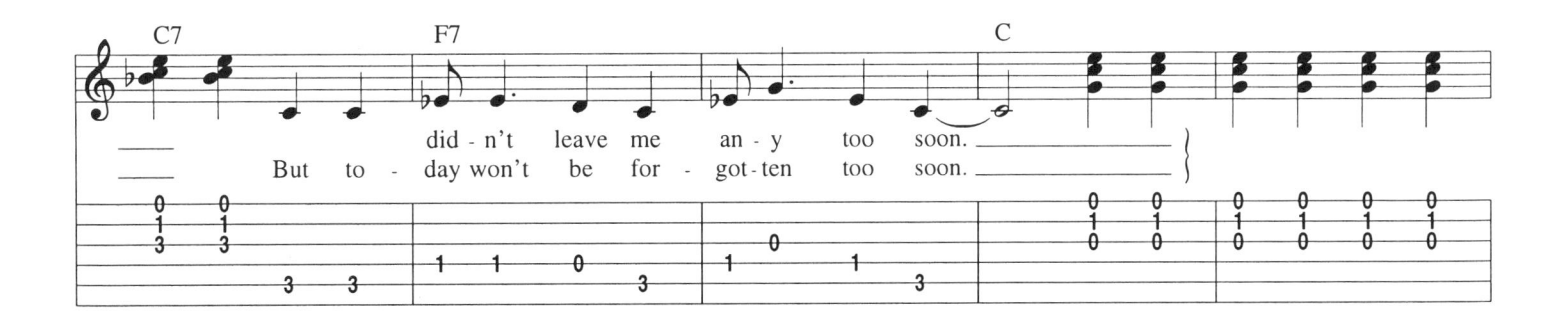

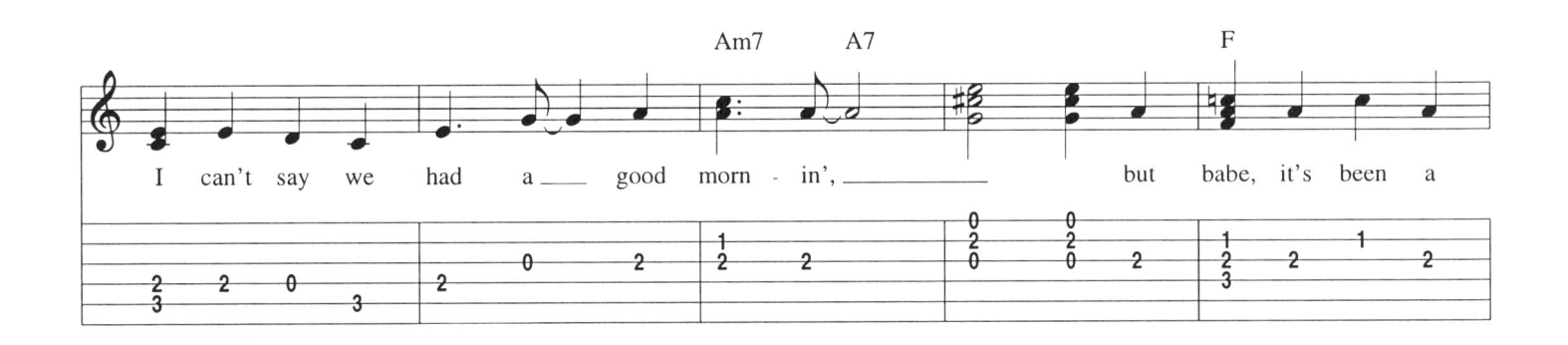

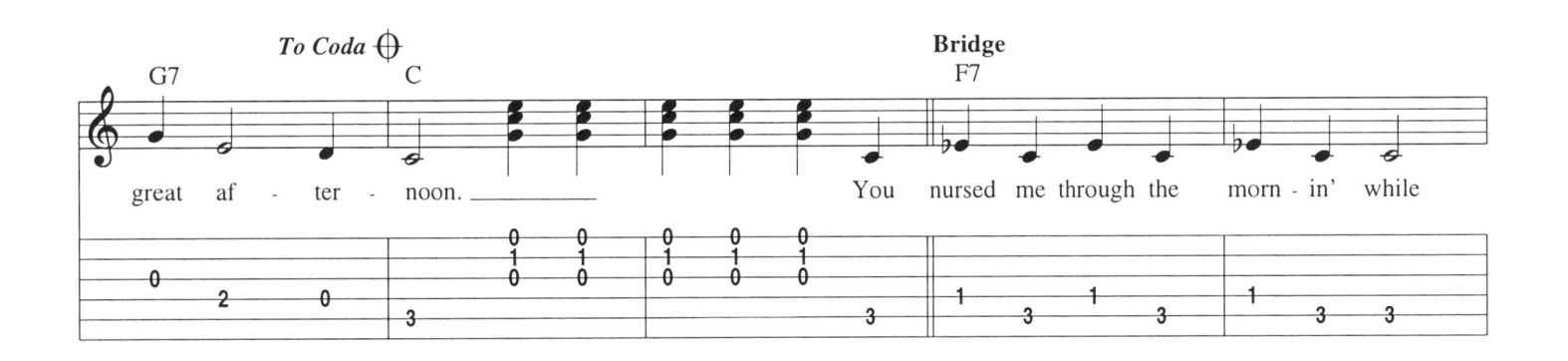

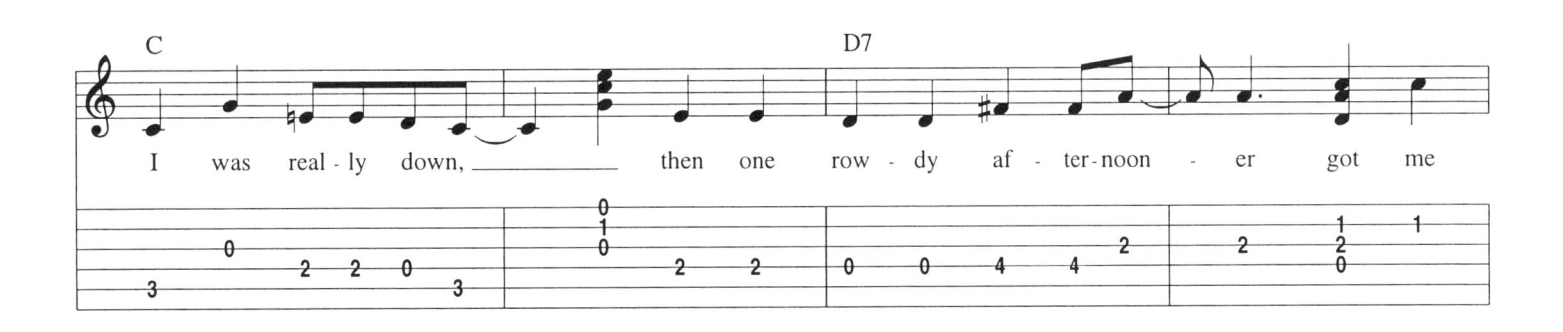

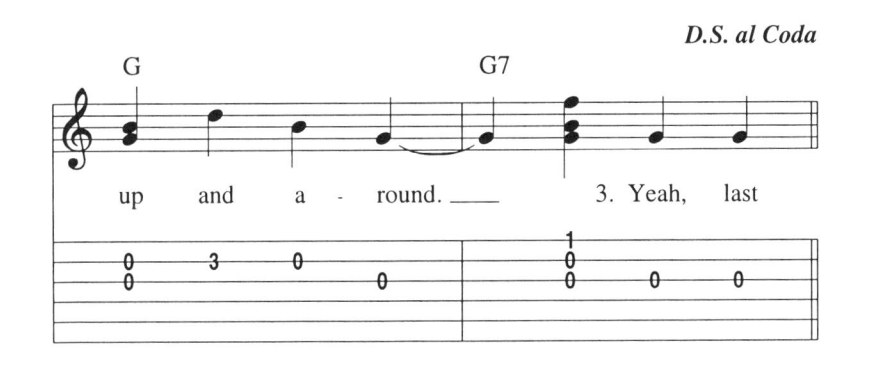

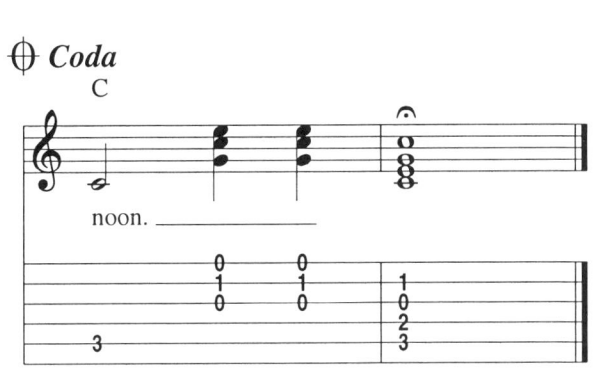

didn't leave me any too soon.
But today won't be forgotten too soon.

I can't say we had a good mornin', but babe, it's been a great afternoon. You nursed me through the mornin' while I was really down, then one rowdy afternoon-er got me up and around. 3. Yeah, last noon.

Let's Chase Each Other Around the Room

Words and Music by Merle Haggard, Freddy Powers and Sheril Rodgers

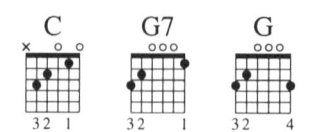

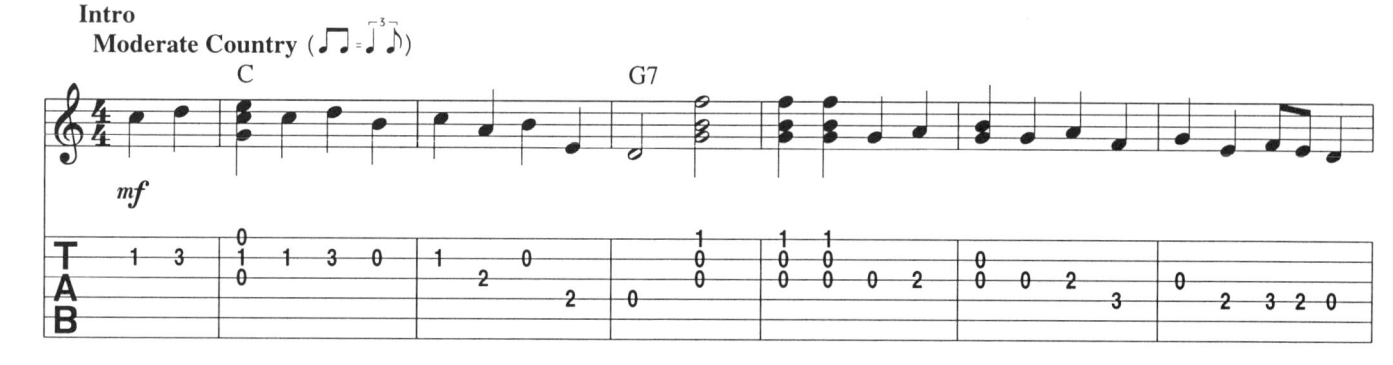

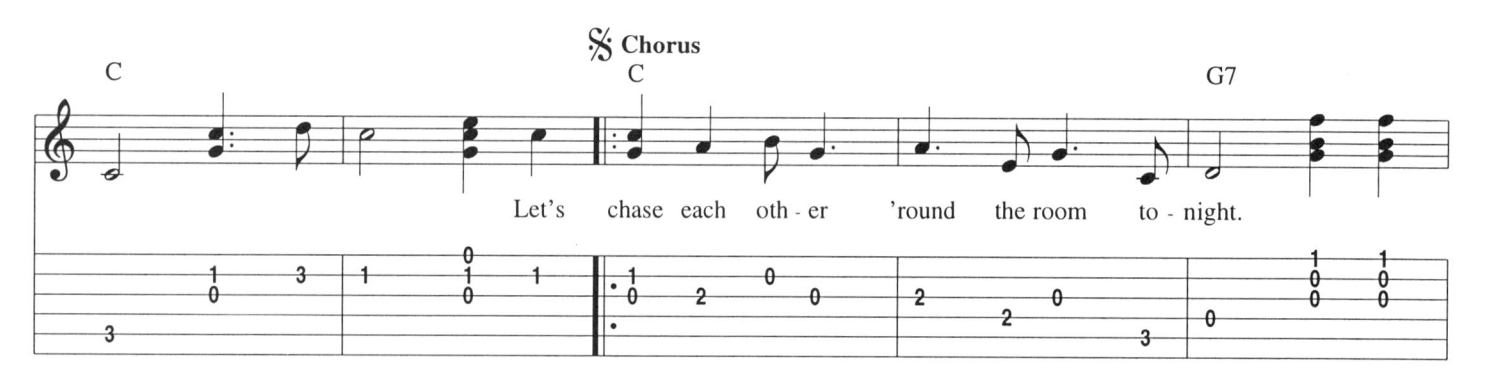

Strum Pattern: 3
Pick Pattern: 3

Intro
Moderate Country

Chorus

Let's chase each oth-er 'round the room to-night.

Let's play the games we played on our wed-ding night.

To lock and bolt the door is on-ly right.

Copyright © 1984 Sony/ATV Songs LLC
All Rights Administered by Sony/ATV Music Publishing, 8 Music Square West, Nashville, TN 37203
International Copyright Secured All Rights Reserved

Lyrics

Let's chase each other 'round the room tonight.

1. Seems like lately people love to play with fire, and the other games they play are just as bad. I'd rather stay at home and feel your burning lips, and play the kind of games that make me glad. Whoa, let's Whoa, let's ... night.

Additional Lyrics

2. Let's don't chase around and make each other weary,
Let's keep all our love at home and out of sight.
Let's leave ev'rything like jealousy behind us,
And let's chase each other 'round the room tonight.

Mama Tried

Words and Music by Merle Haggard

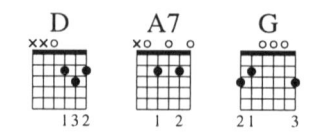

D A7 G

Strum Pattern: 3, 4
Pick Pattern: 1, 3

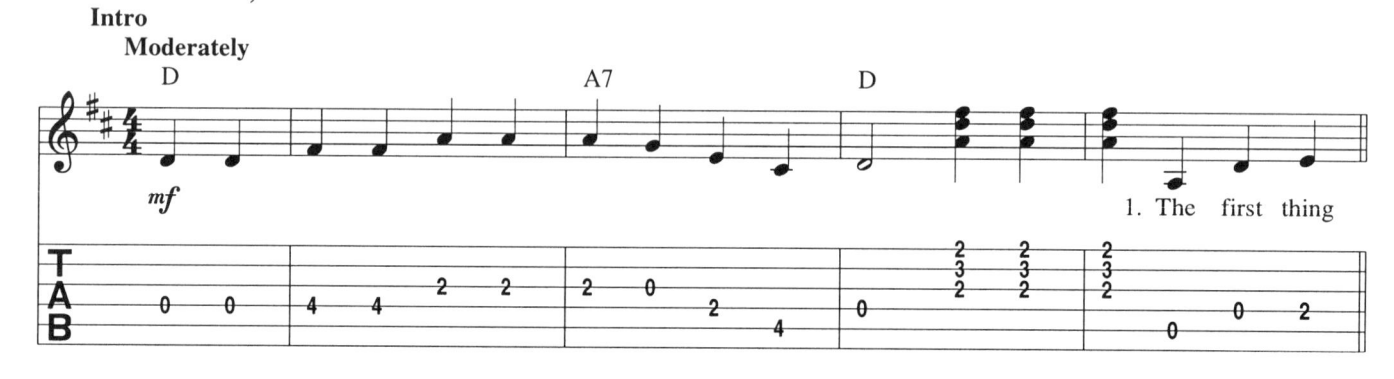

Intro
Moderately

1. The first thing I re-mem-ber know-in' was a lone-some whis-tle blow-in', and a young-on's dream of grow-in' up to ride, on a freight train leav-in' town, not know-in' where I'm bound, and no

---

Copyright © 1968 Sony/ATV Songs LLC
Copyright Renewed
All Rights Administered by Sony/ATV Music Publishing, 8 Music Square West, Nashville, TN 37203
International Copyright Secured   All Rights Reserved

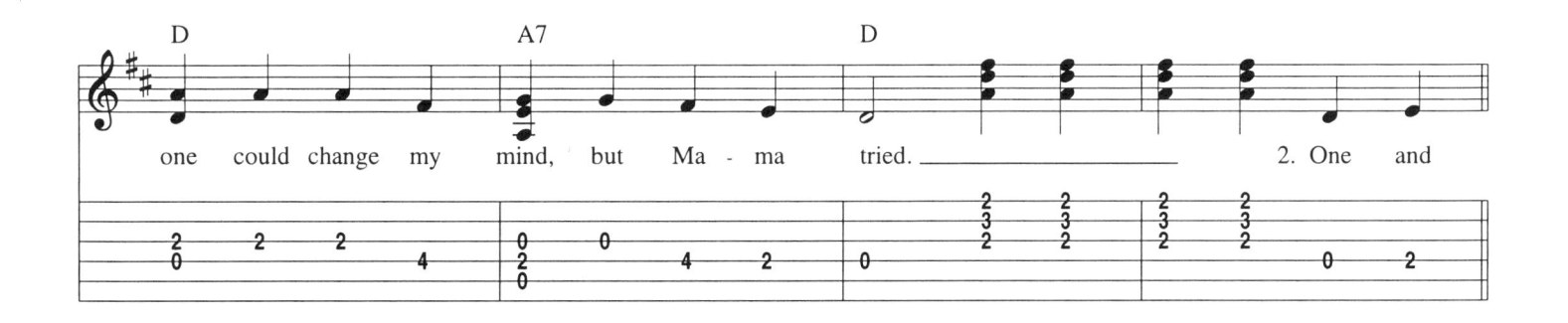

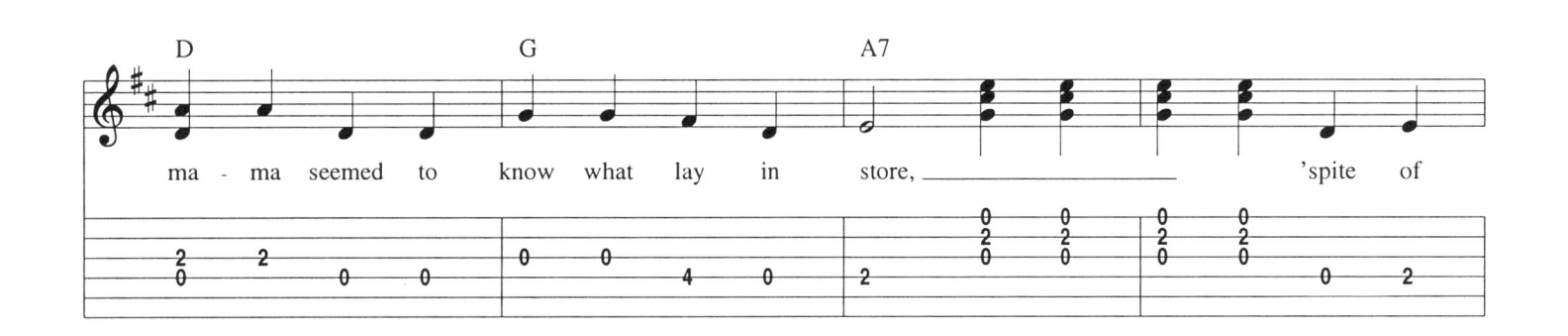

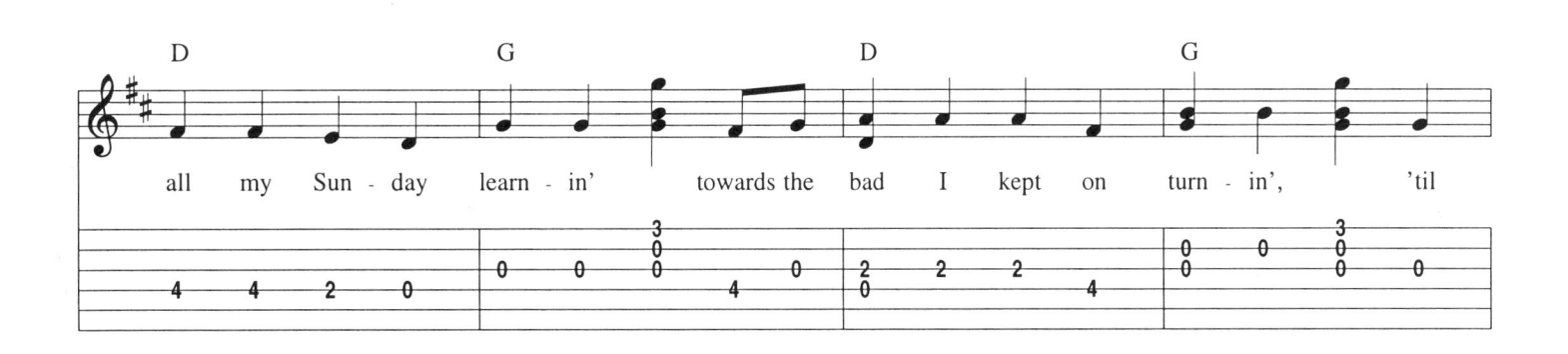

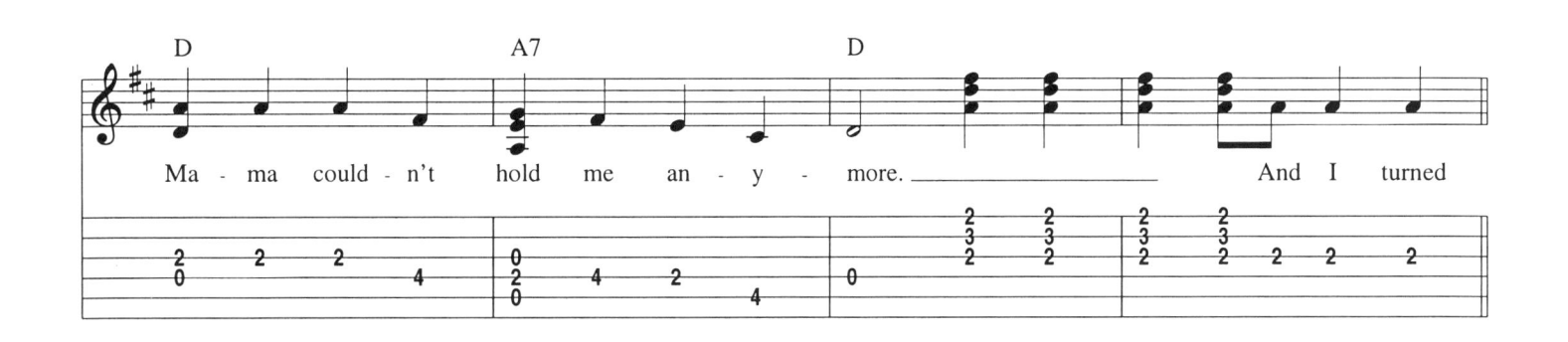

one could change my mind, but Mama tried. 2. One and

Verse

only rebel child, from a fam'ly meek and mild, my

3. *See Additional Lyrics*

mama seemed to know what lay in store, 'spite of

all my Sunday learnin' towards the bad I kept on turnin', 'til

Mama couldn't hold me anymore. And I turned

Chorus

twen-ty-one in pris-on do-in' life with-out pa-role, no one could steer me right, but Ma-ma tried, Ma-ma tried. Ma-ma tried to raise me bet-ter, but her plead-ing I de-nied. That leaves on-ly me to blame, 'cause Ma-ma tried. 3. Dear ol' tried.

Additional Lyrics

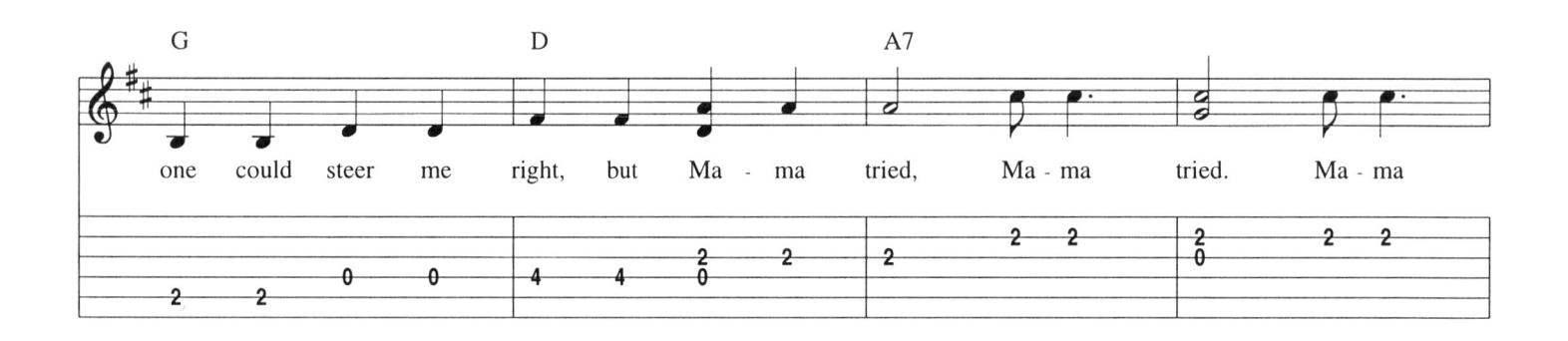

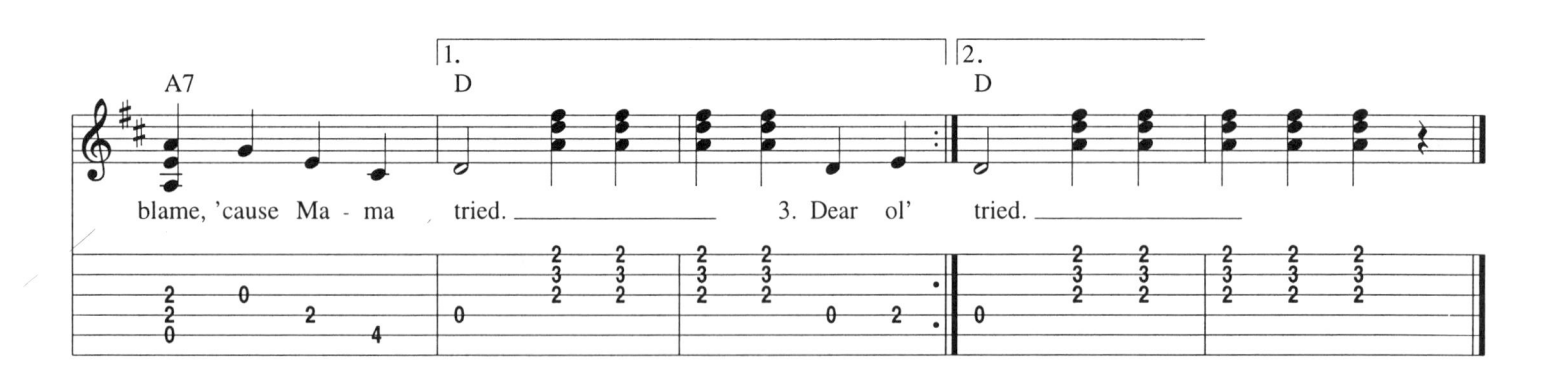

3. Dear ol' Daddy, rest his soul,
   Left my mom a heavy load.
   She tried so very hard to fill his shoes,
   Workin' hours without rest,
   Wanted me to have the best.
   She tried to raise me right but I refused.

Misery and Gin

Words and Music by John Durrill and Snuff Garrett

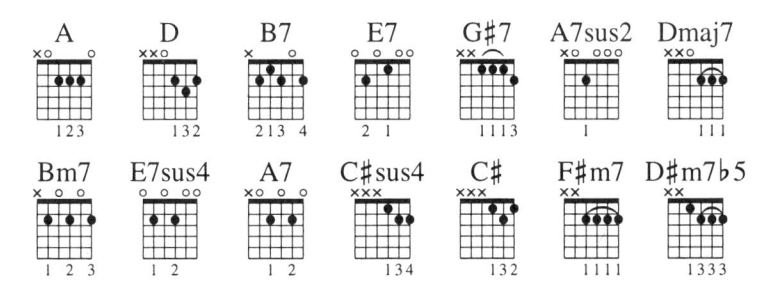

Strum Pattern: 3, 4
Pick Pattern: 1, 3

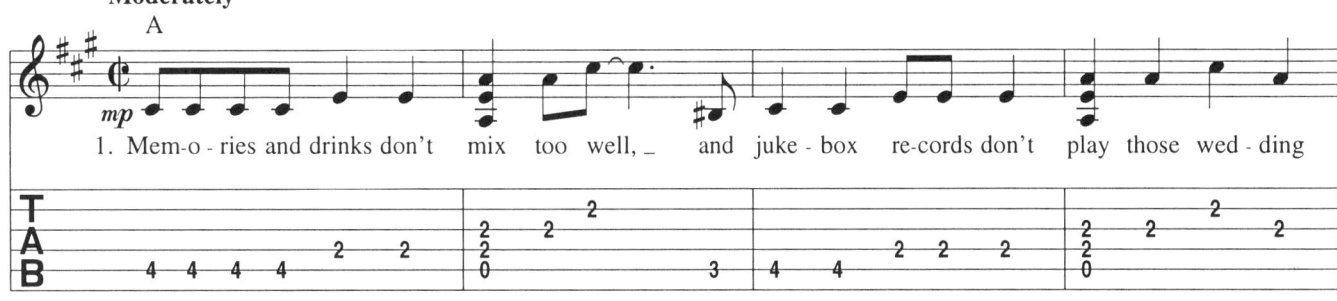

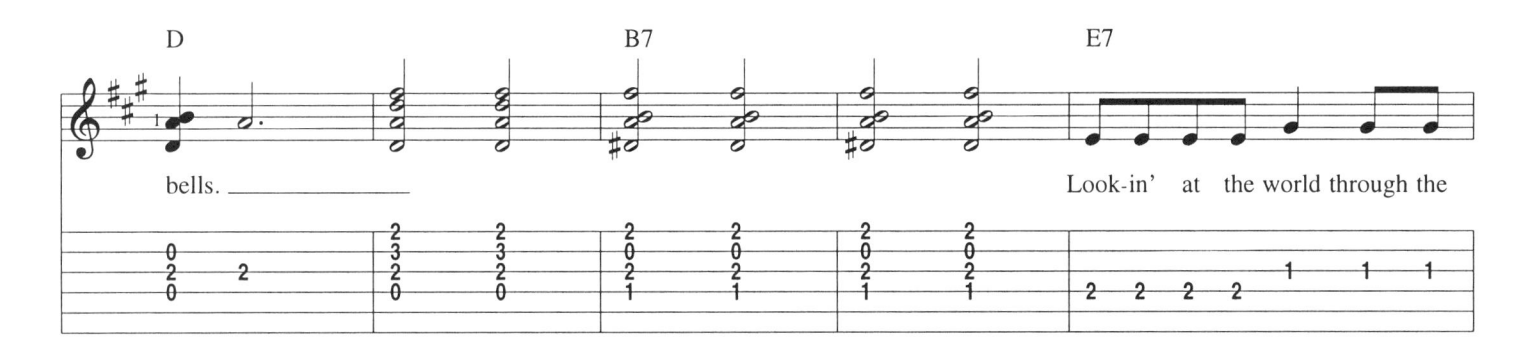

Verse
Moderately

1. Mem-o-ries and drinks don't mix too well, and juke-box re-cords don't play those wed-ding bells.

Look-in' at the world through the bot-tom of a glass, all I see is a man who's fad-in' fast.

2. To-night I need a wom-an a-gain.
3. *See Additional Lyrics*

Copyright © 1980 by Careers-BMG Music Publishing, Inc.
International Copyright Secured All Rights Reserved

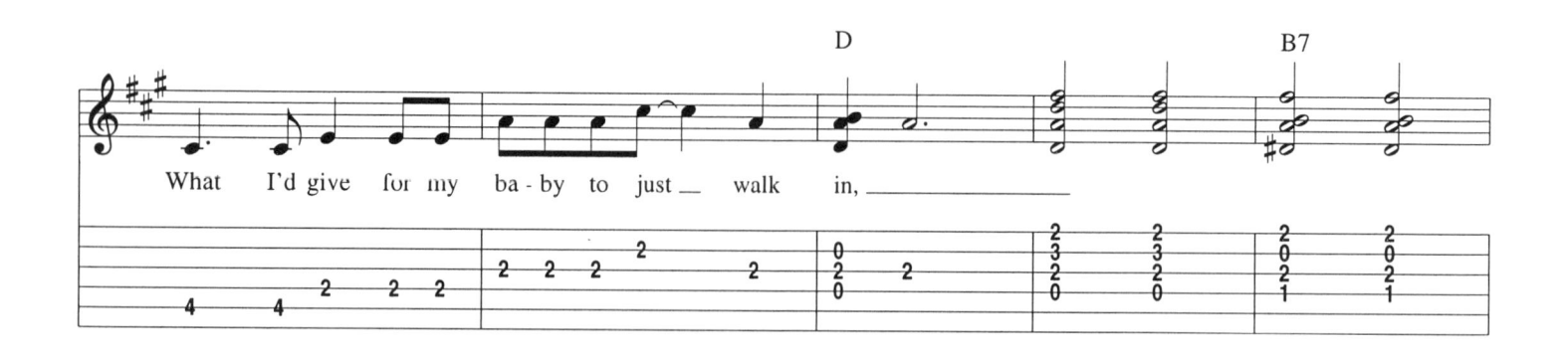

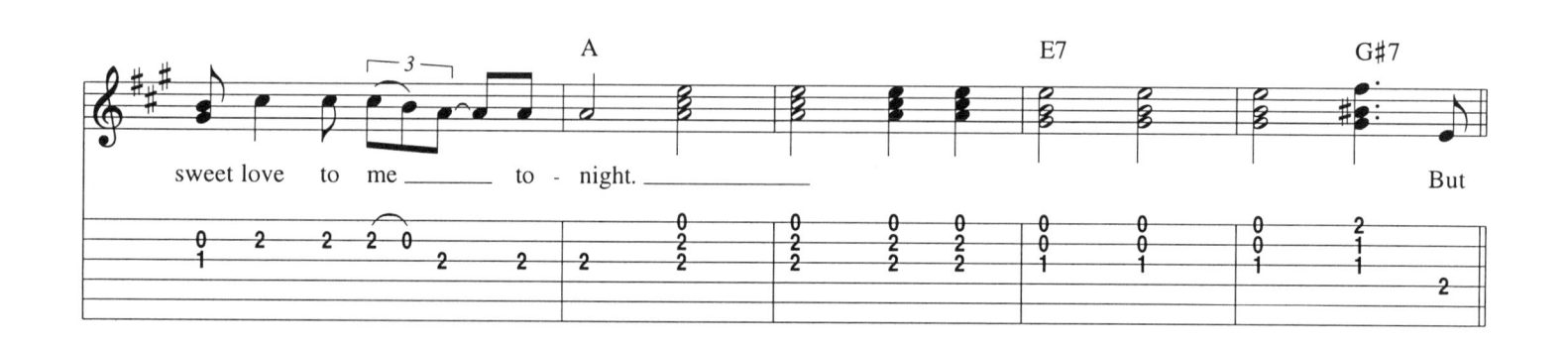

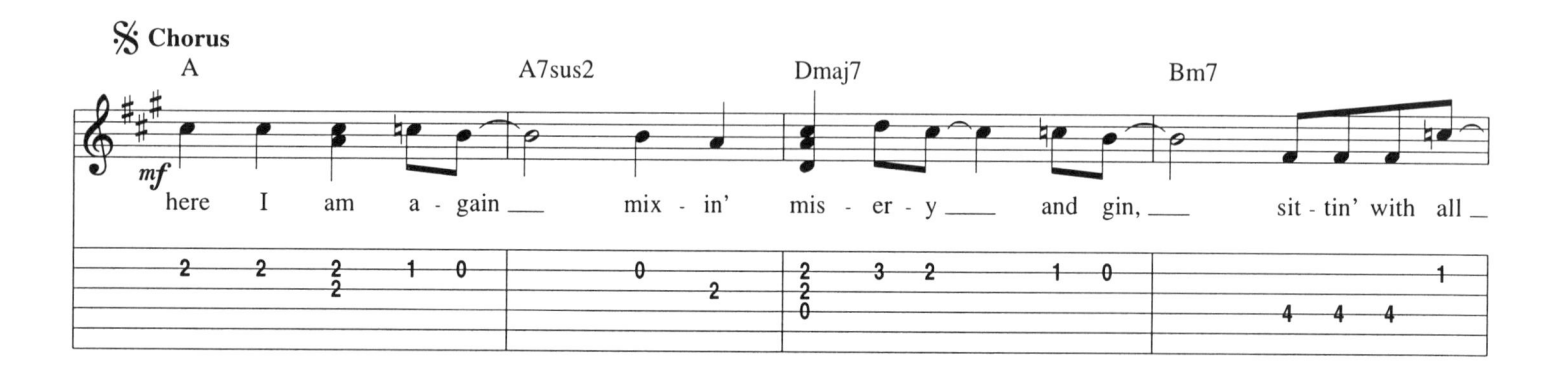

What I'd give for my ba-by to just walk in, [D] [B7]

Sit down be-side me and say it's al-right, [E7] take me home and make

sweet love to me to-night. [A] [E7] [G#7] But

𝄋 Chorus

here I am a-gain [A] mix-in' [A7sus2] mis-er-y [Dmaj7] and gin, sit-tin' with all [Bm7]

my friends and talk-in' [E7sus4] to my-self; [A] I [A7]

Lyrics under the staves:

look like I'm hav-ing a good time but an-y fool can tell

that this hon-ky tonk heav-en real-ly makes you feel

like hell. 3. I

feel like hell.

Additional Lyrics

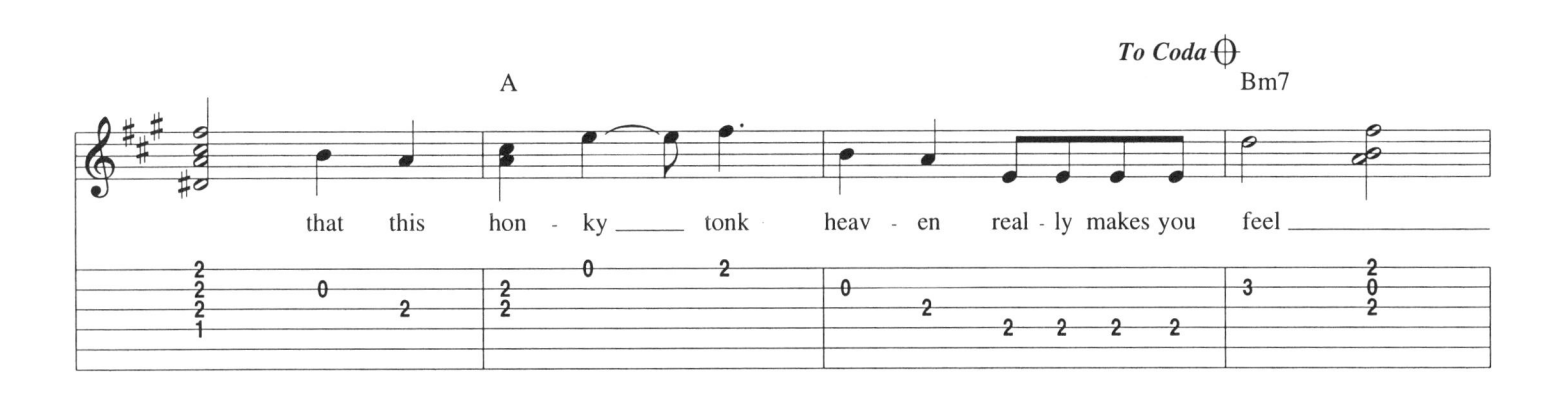

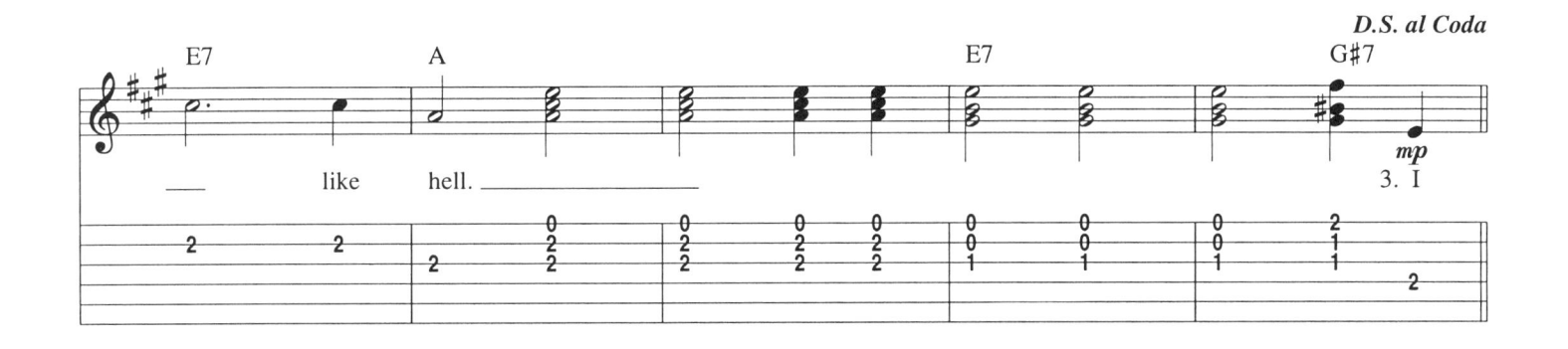

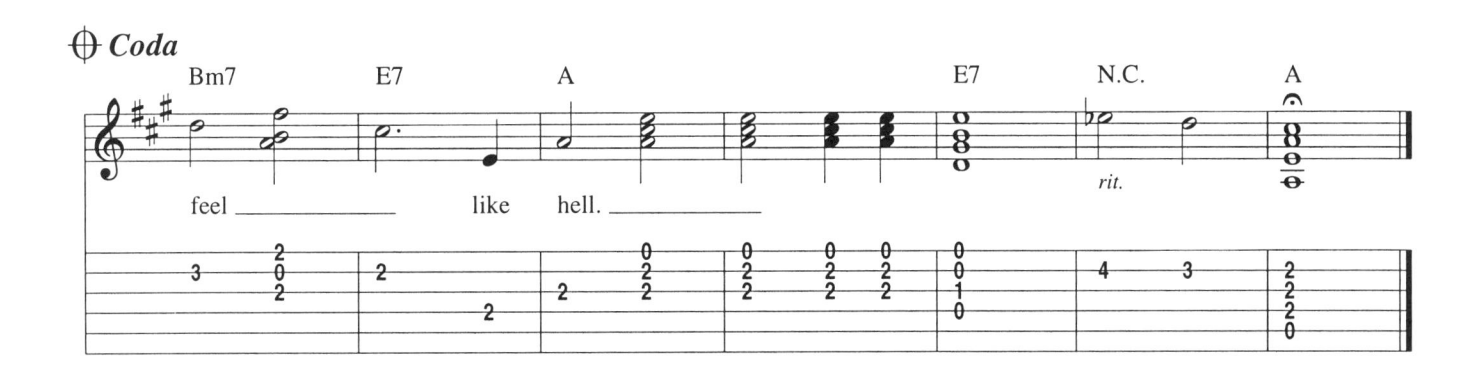

3. I light a lonely woman's cigarette
   And we start talkin' about what we wanna forget.
   Her life story and mine are the same,
   We both lost someone and only have ourselves to blame.

My Favorite Memory

Words and Music by Merle Haggard

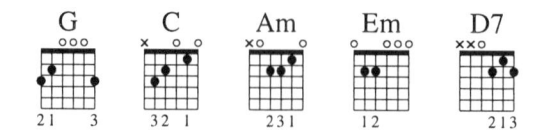

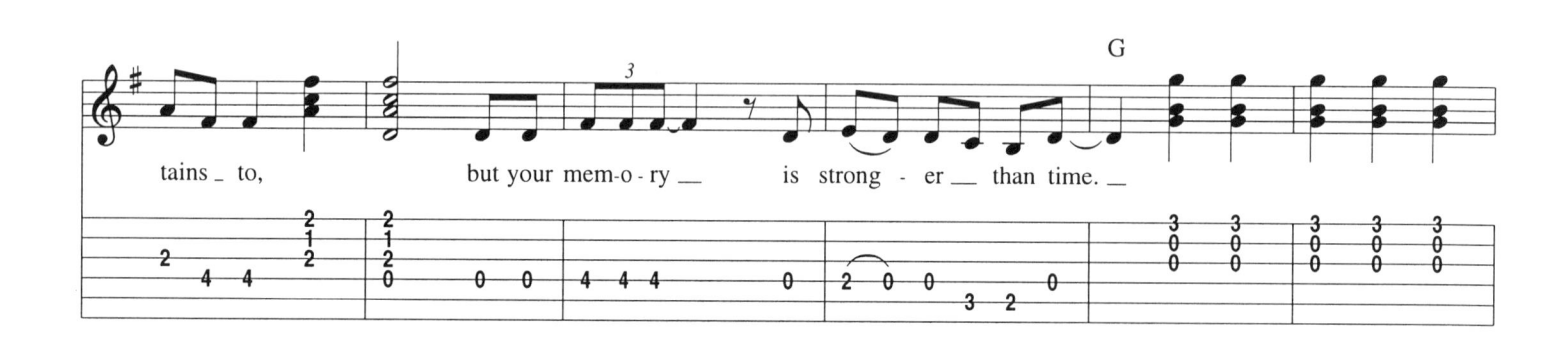

Chords: G, C, Am, Em, D7

Strum Pattern: 8, 9
Pick Pattern: 7, 8

Verse
Flowing

1. The first time we met ___ is a fav - o - rite ___ mem - 'ry ___ of mine. ___

They say time ___ chang - es all _____ it per - tains _ to, but your mem-o-ry ___ is strong - er ___ than time. ___

I guess ev - 'ry - thing _ does change ___ ex - cept what you

Copyright © 1981 Sony/ATV Songs LLC
All Rights Administered by Sony/ATV Music Publishing, 8 Music Square West, Nashville, TN 37203
International Copyright Secured All Rights Reserved

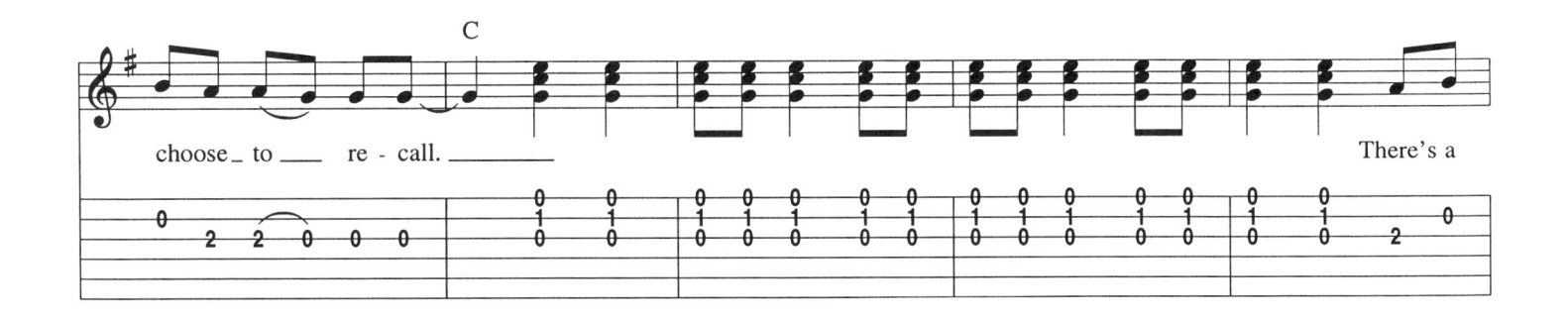

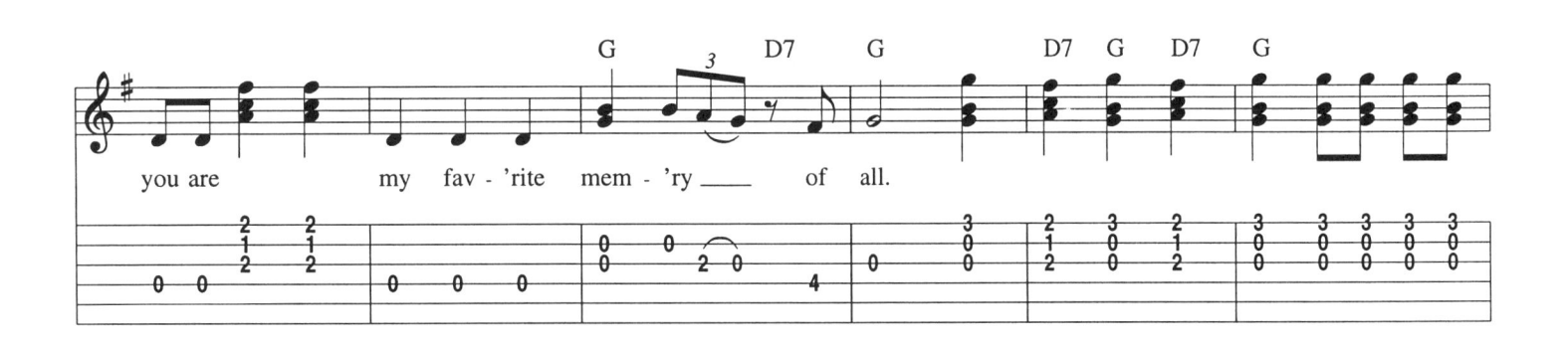

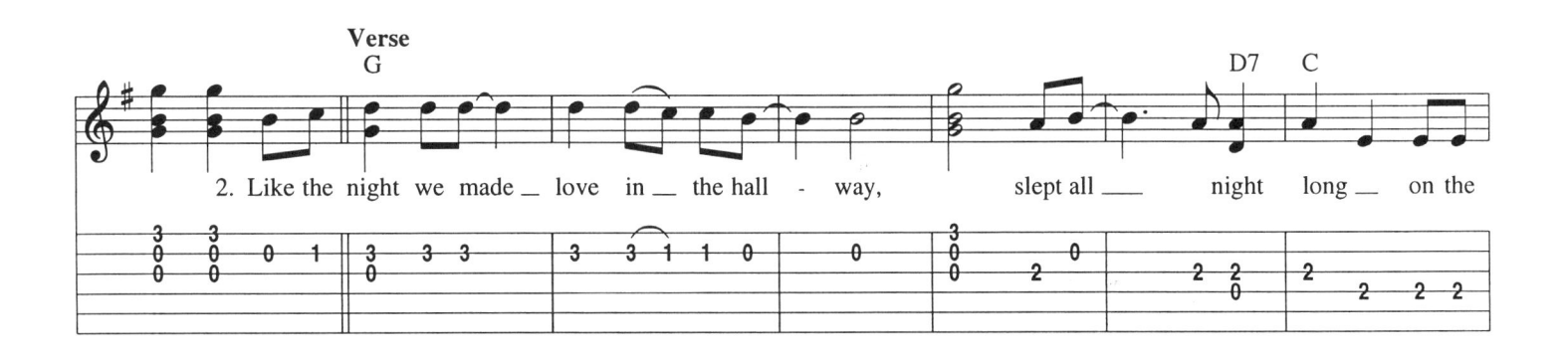

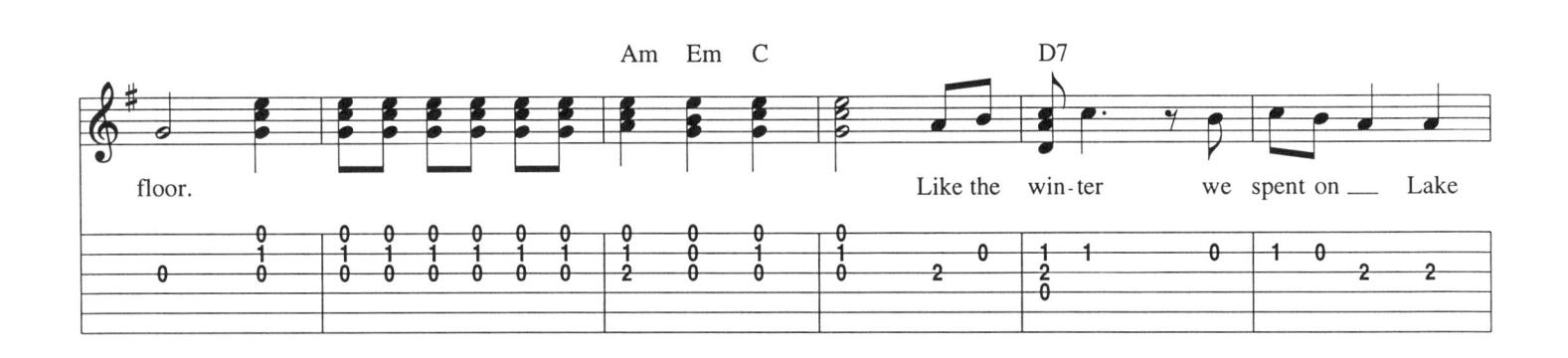

choose to re-call. There's a mil-lion good day-dreams to dream on but, ba-by, you are my fav-'rite mem-'ry of all.

Verse

2. Like the night we made love in the hall-way, slept all night long on the floor. Like the win-ter we spent on Lake

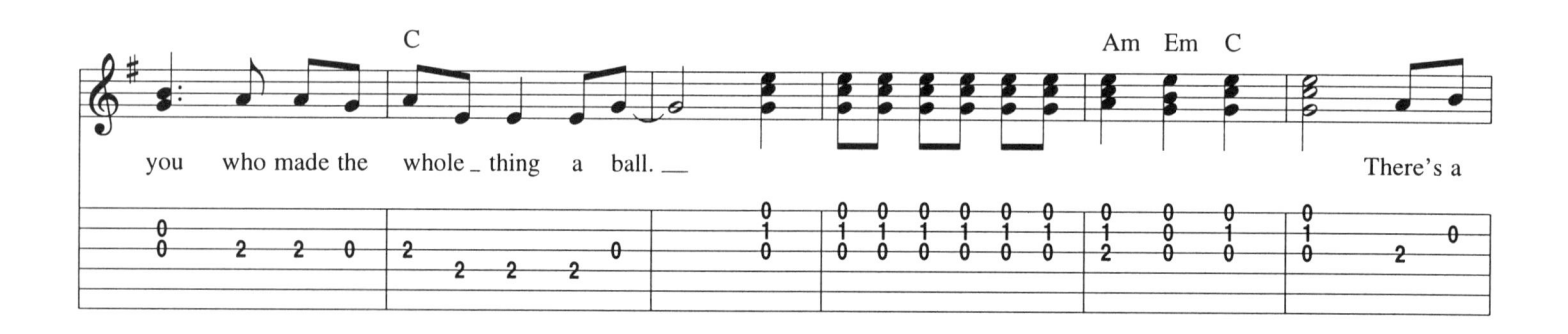

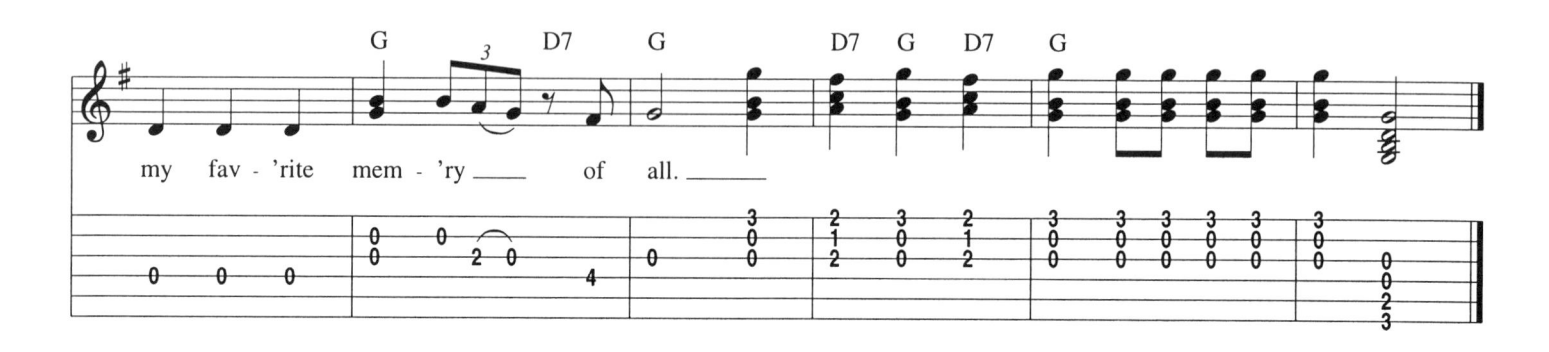

Shas-ta a-lone, and clos-er than ev-er be-fore. And I re-mem-ber that London va-ca-tion. It was you who made the whole thing a ball. There's a mil-lion good times I could dwell on, but, ba-by, you are my fav-'rite mem-'ry of all.

Rainbow Stew

Words and Music by Merle Haggard

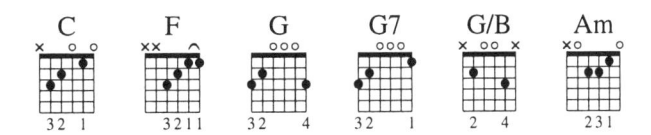

Chords: C, F, G, G7, G/B, Am

Strum Pattern: 3
Pick Pattern: 3

Verse
Easy Country Swing ($\sqrt{} = \sqrt{}^3\sqrt{}$)

1. There's a big brown cloud in the city and the country-side's a sin. The price of life is too high to give up, it's gotta come down again. When world-wide war is over and done and the dream of peace comes true, we'll all be drinkin' that free Bubble Up and eatin' that rainbow stew.

3. *See Additional Lyrics*

2. When they

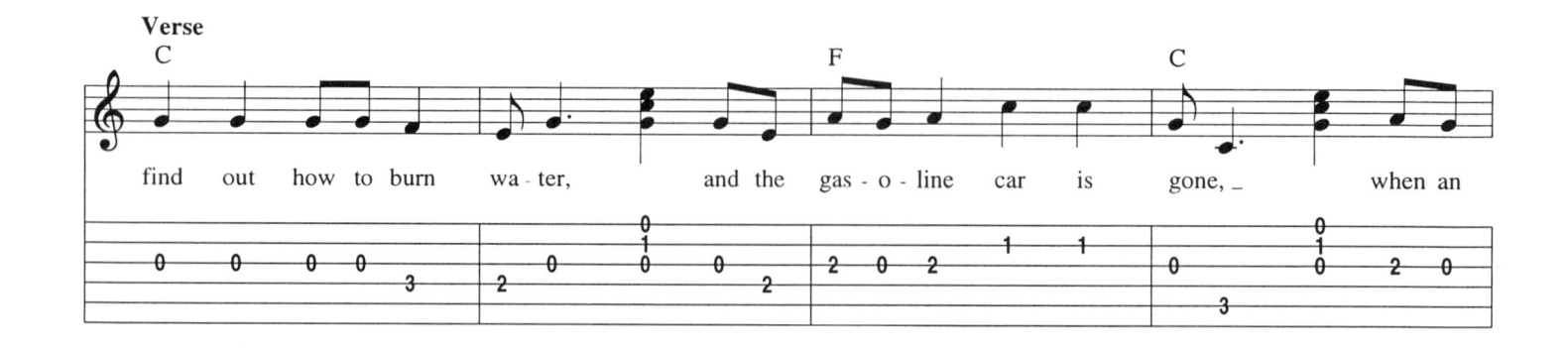

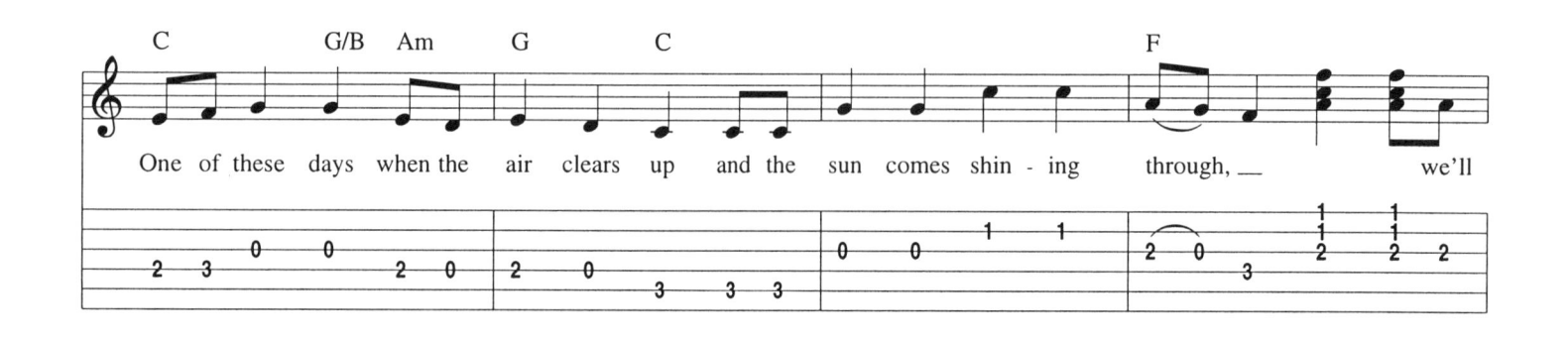

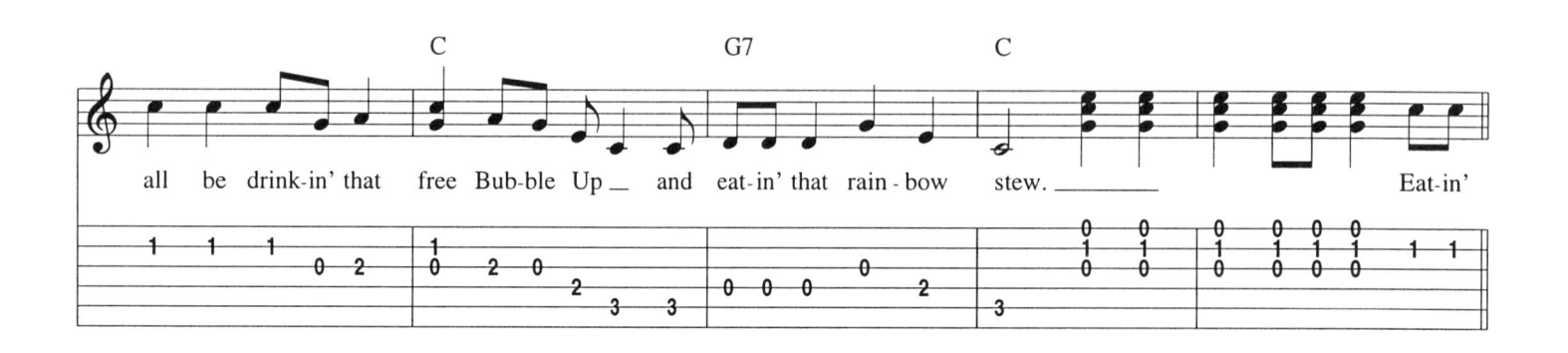

Verse

find out how to burn water, and the gas-o-line car is gone, when an air-plane flies without an-y fuel and the sun-light heats our homes.

One of these days when the air clears up and the sun comes shin-ing through, we'll all be drink-in' that free Bub-ble Up and eat-in' that rain-bow stew. Eat-in'

Chorus

rain-bow stew in a sil-ver spoon, un-der-neath those skies of blue; we'll

Additional Lyrics

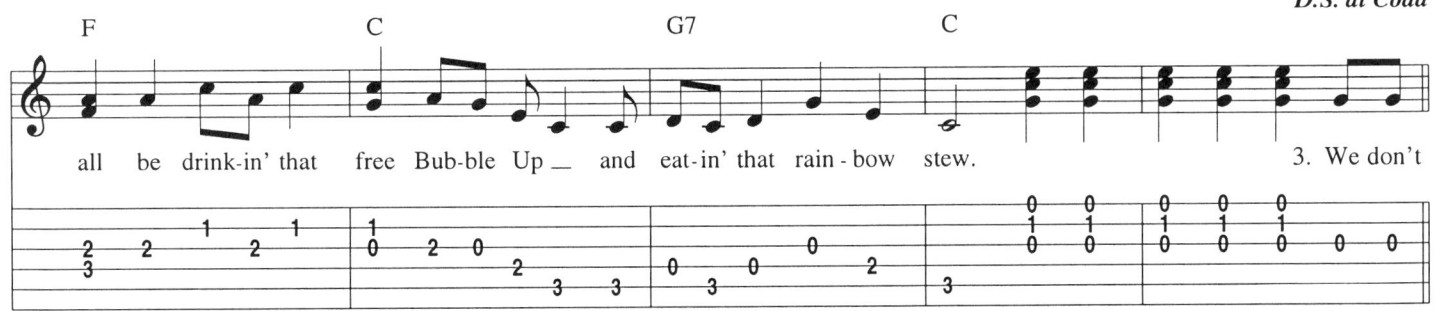

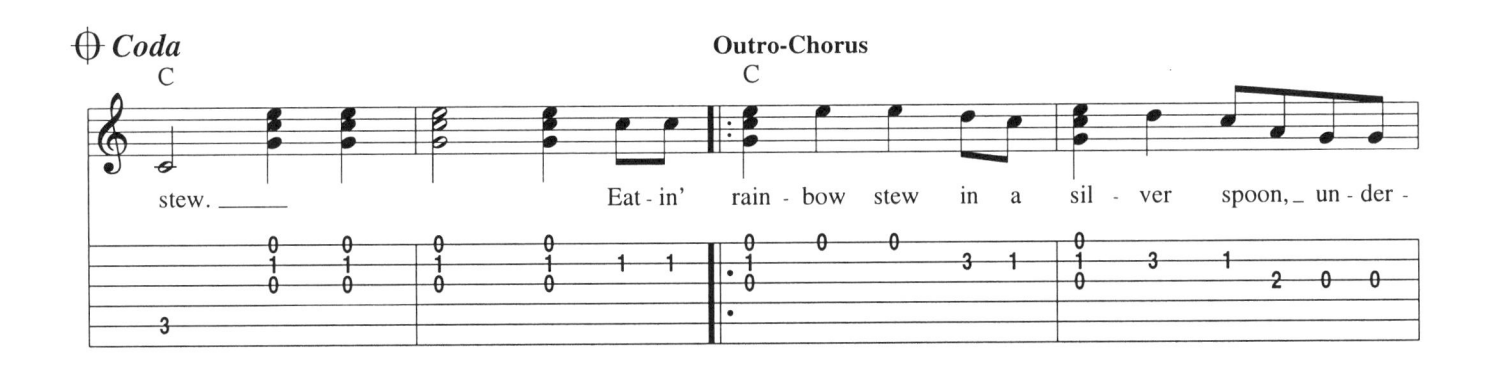

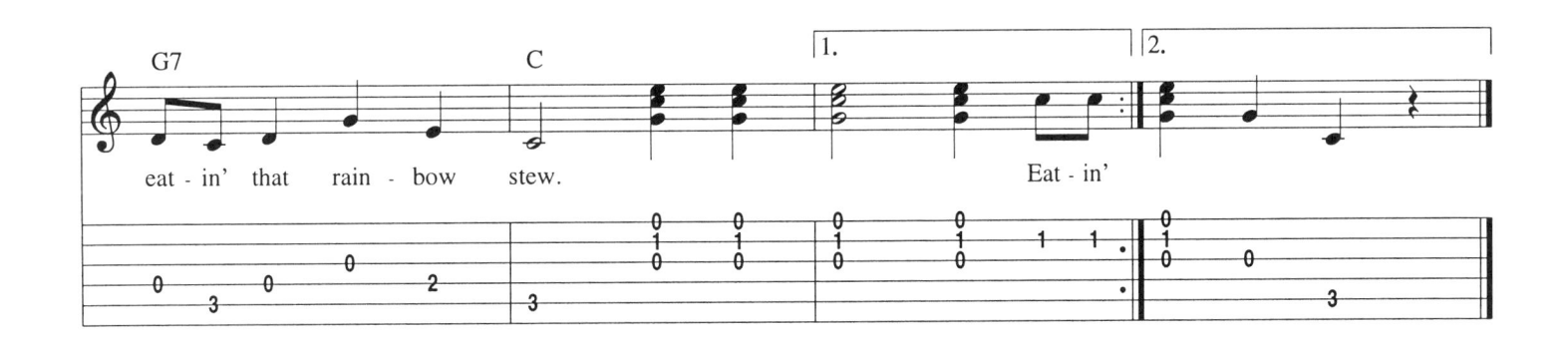

3. We don't have to get high to get happy,
   Just think about what's in store.
   When we all start doin' what we all start doin',
   We won't be hungry no more.
   When a president goes through the White House door
   And does what he says he'll do,
   We'll all be drinkin' that free Bubble Up
   And eatin' that rainbow stew.

Okie From Muskogee

Words and Music by Merle Haggard and Roy Edward Burris

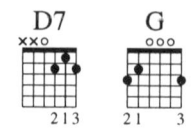

D7 G

Strum Pattern: 3, 4
Pick Pattern: 1, 3

Intro
Moderately Fast

1. We don't smoke mar-i-jua-na in Mus-ko-gee, ___ and we don't take our
2., 3. *See Additional Lyrics*

trips on L. S. D. And we don't burn our draft cards down on

Main Street, but we like liv-ing right and be-ing free. ___

Copyright © 1969 Sony/ATV Songs LLC
Copyright Renewed
All Rights Administered by Sony/ATV Music Publishing, 8 Music Square West, Nashville, TN 37203
International Copyright Secured All Rights Reserved

Chorus

And I'm proud to be an O-kie from Mus-ko-gee; _____ a place where e-ven squares can have a ball. _____ We still wave Ol' Glo-ry down at the Court House, white light-ning's still the big-gest thrill of all. _____

3. Leath-er _____

Additional Lyrics

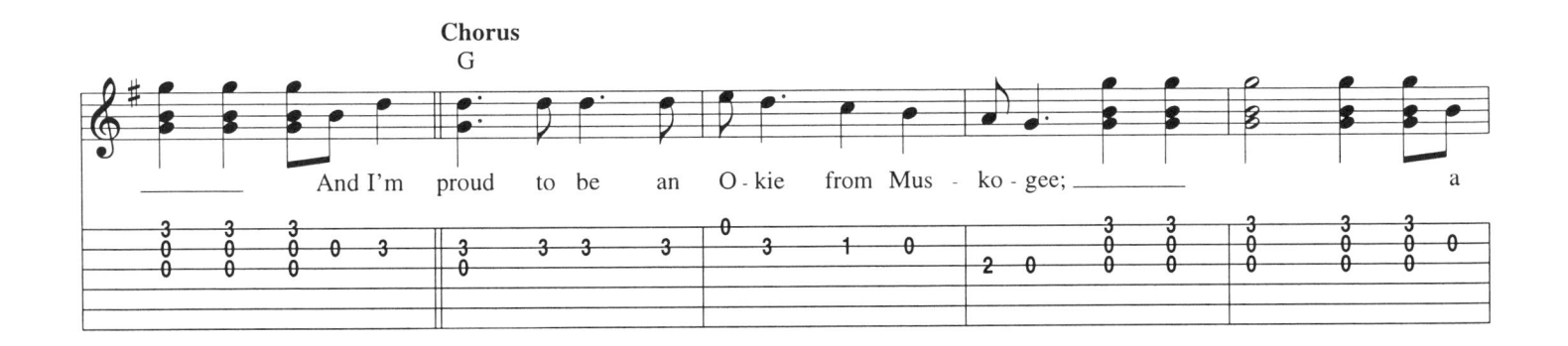

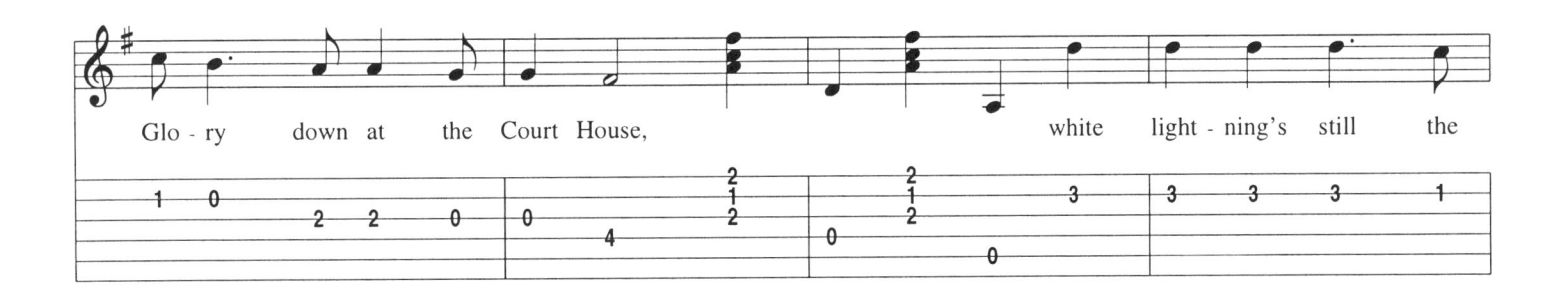

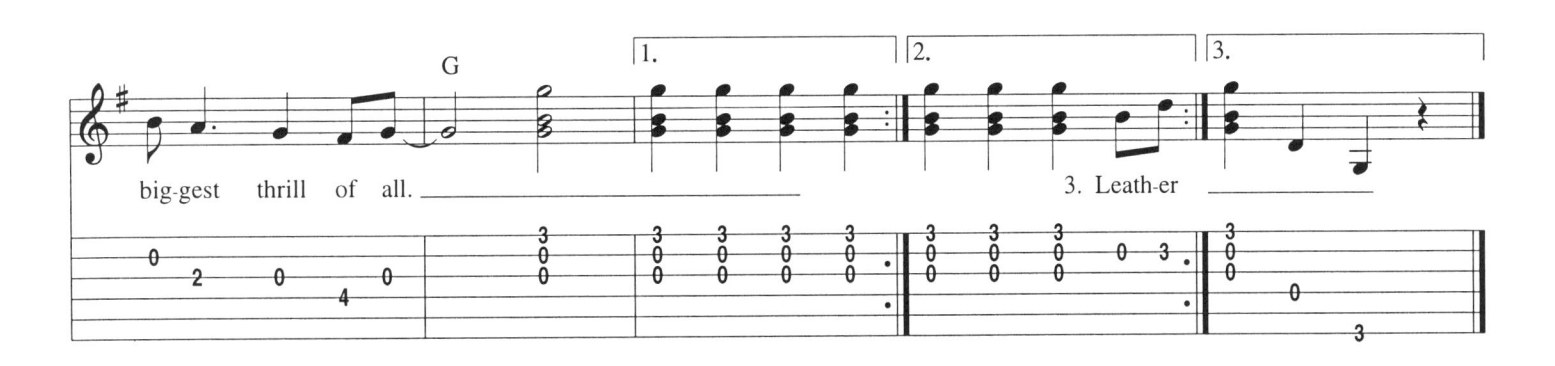

2. We don't make a party out of loving,
   But we like holding hands and pitching woo.
   We don't let our hair grow long and shaggy
   Like the hippies out in San Francisco do.

3. Leather boots are still in style if a man needs footwear,
   Beads and Roman sandals won't be seen.
   Football's still the roughest thing on campus,
   And the kids here still respect the College Dean.

A Place to Fall Apart

Words and Music by Merle Haggard, Willie Nelson and Freddy Powers

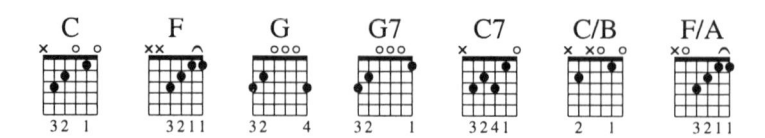

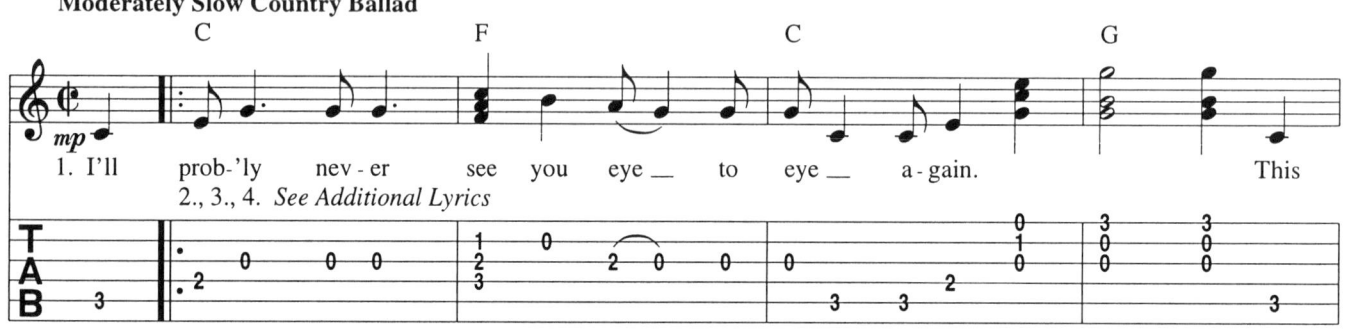

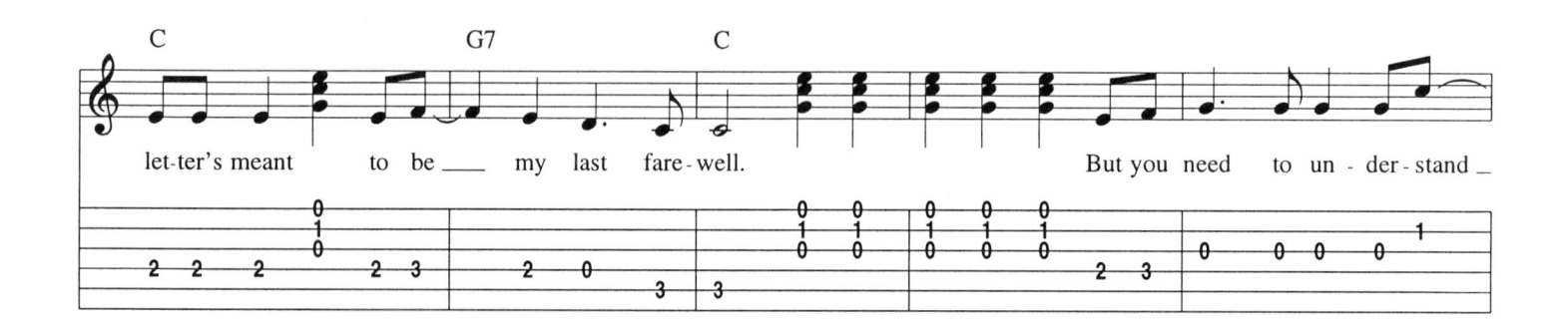

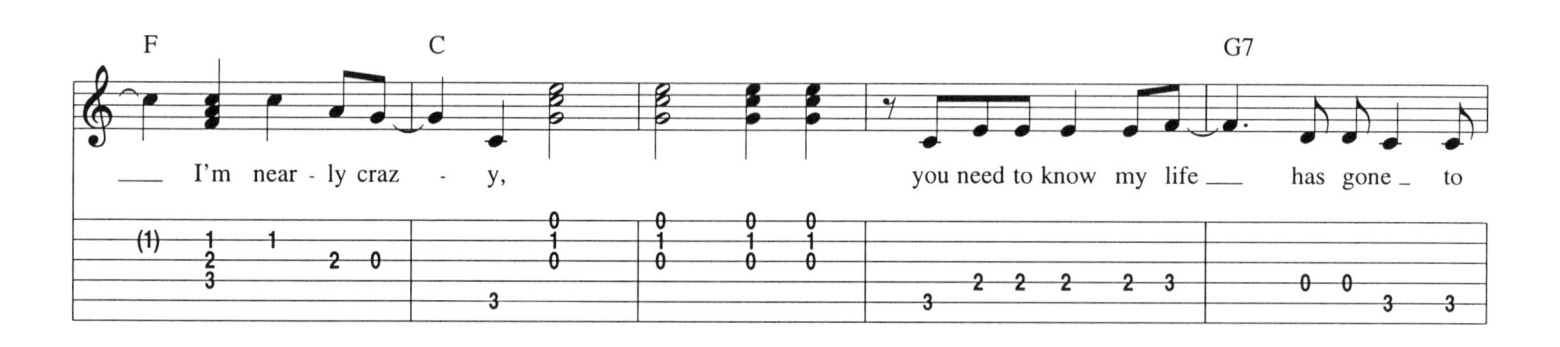

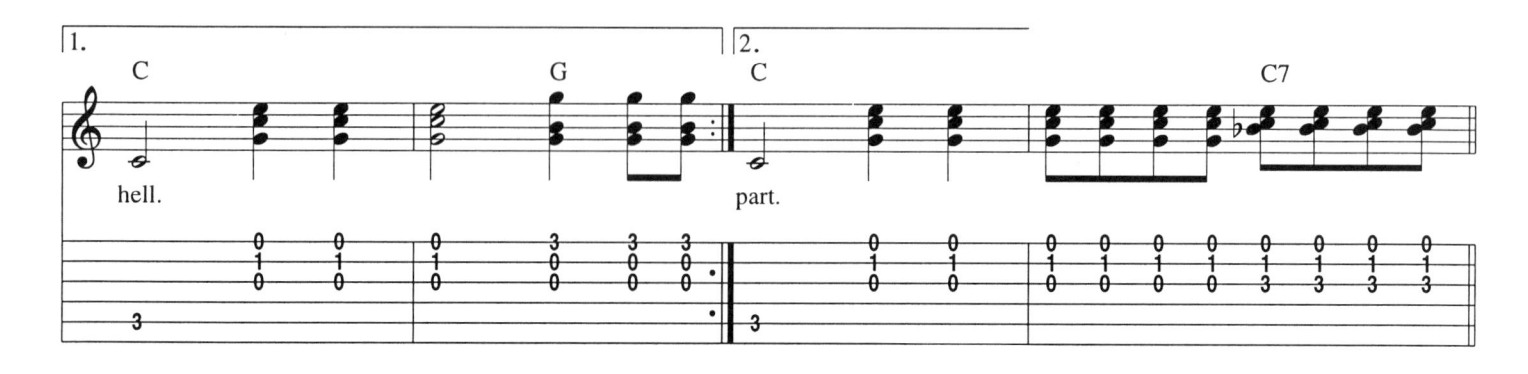

Chords: C F G G7 C7 C/B F/A

Strum Pattern: 3, 4
Pick Pattern: 1, 3

Verse
Moderately Slow Country Ballad

1. I'll prob-'ly nev-er see you eye to eye a-gain. This let-ter's meant to be my last fare-well. But you need to un-der-stand I'm near-ly craz-y, you need to know my life has gone to hell.

(2., 3., 4. See Additional Lyrics)

1. part.

Chorus

mf Look-ing for a place to fall a-part.

Try'n' to find a place that I can leave my heart.

need to be some-where hid-in' when I feel the tear-drops start.

To Coda
D.S. al Coda (take repeat)

Look-in' for a place to fall a-part.

Coda

a-part. Look-in' for a place to fall a-part.

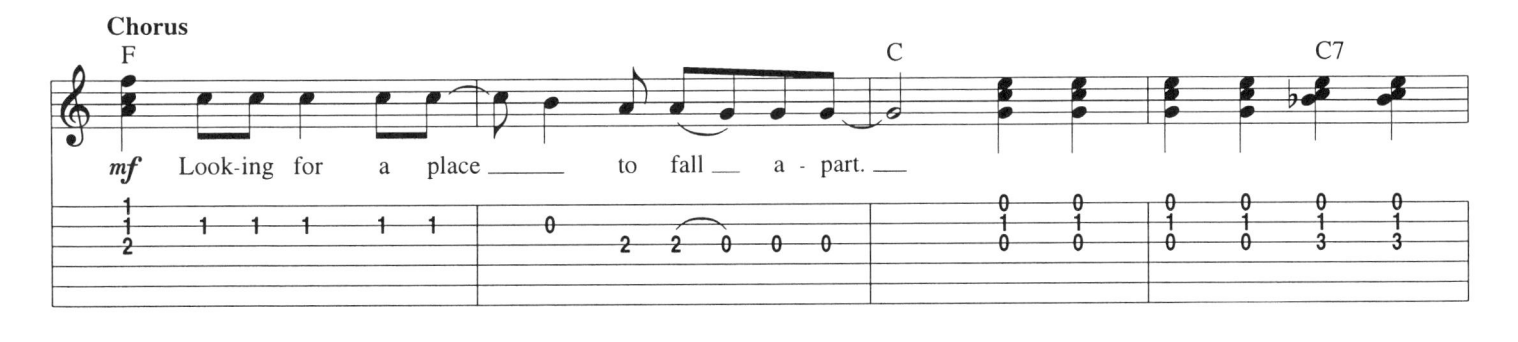

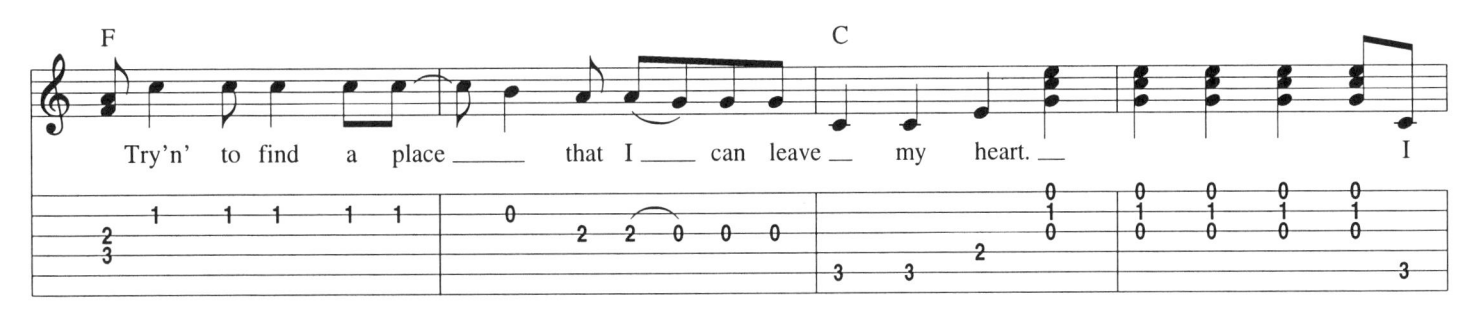

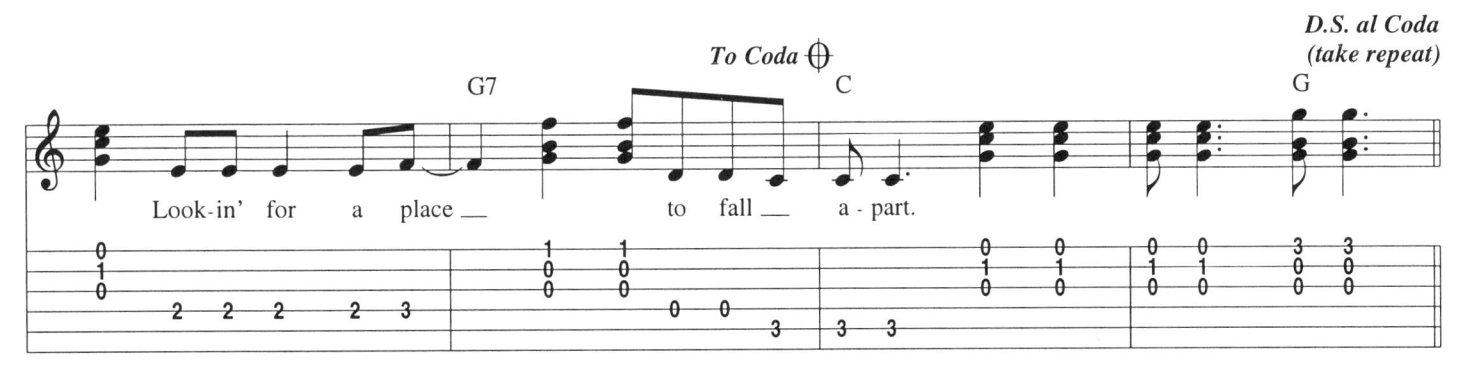

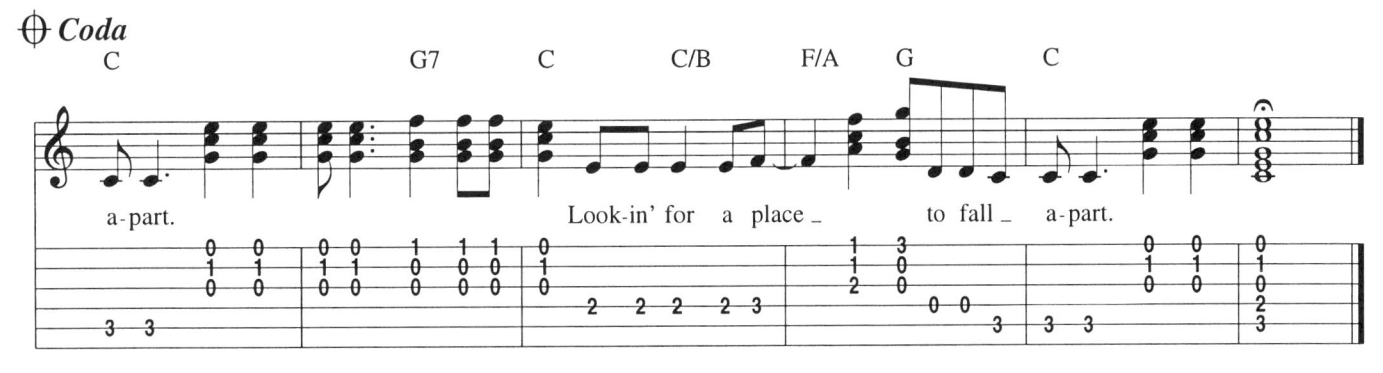

Additional Lyrics

2. Write me back and tell me why it ended,
   Send a letter that I can show my heart.
   I'll be somewhere between I love you and what you're feeling now,
   Lookin' for a place to fall apart.

3. I can't seem to justify your leavin' me,
   I'm bewildered as to how it all came down.
   I thought everything was fine until your phone call,
   The call that turned my world upside down.

4. Send me word and tell me why it ended,
   I need some final proof to show my heart.
   I'll be somewhere between I love you and what you're feelin' now,
   Lookin' for a place to fall apart.

Ramblin' Fever

Words and Music by Merle Haggard

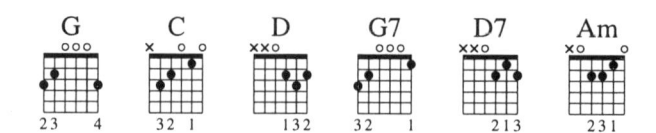

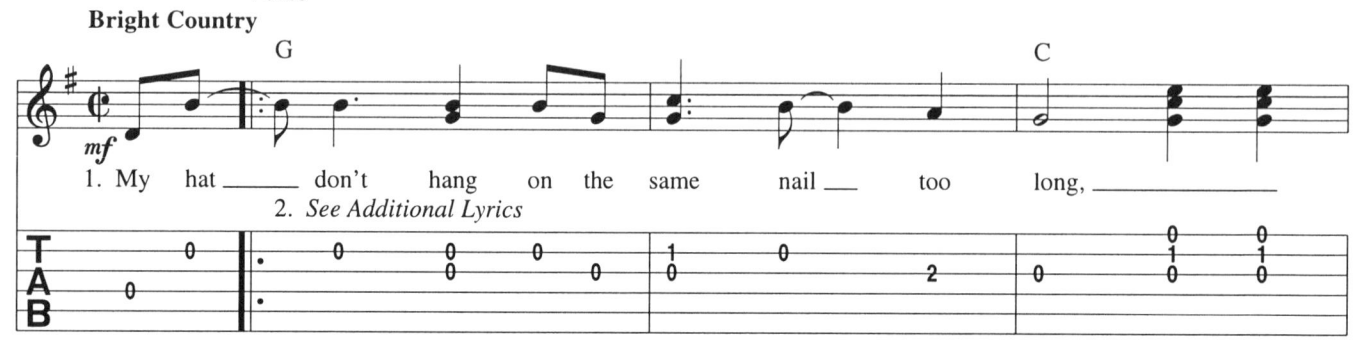

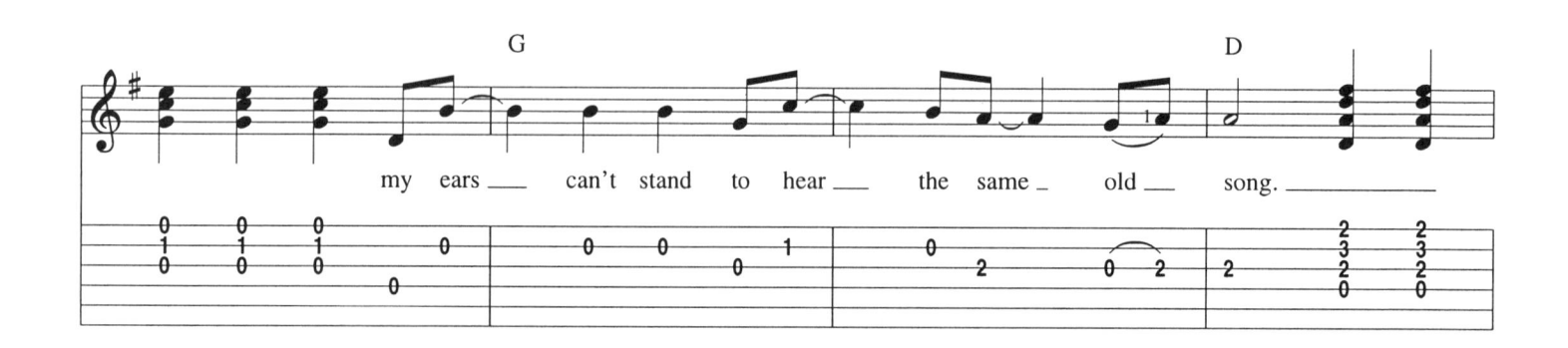

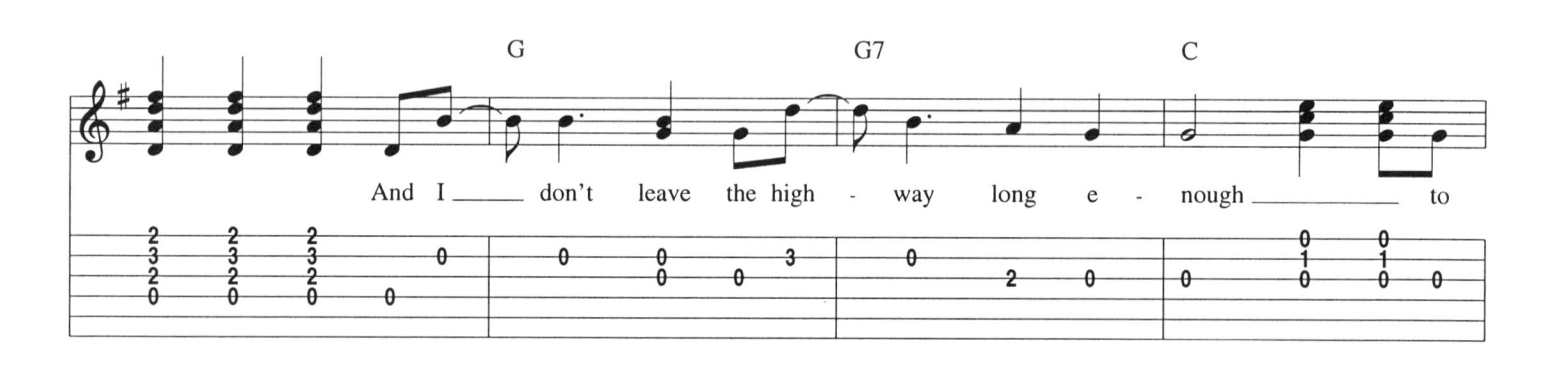

Strum Pattern: 1, 3
Pick Pattern: 3, 4

Bright Country

Verse

1. My hat don't hang on the same nail too long,
2. *See Additional Lyrics*

my ears can't stand to hear the same old song.

And I don't leave the highway long enough to

bog down in the mud, 'cause I've got ramblin'

Copyright © 1977 Sony/ATV Songs LLC
All Rights Administered by Sony/ATV Music Publishing, 8 Music Square West, Nashville, TN 37203
International Copyright Secured   All Rights Reserved

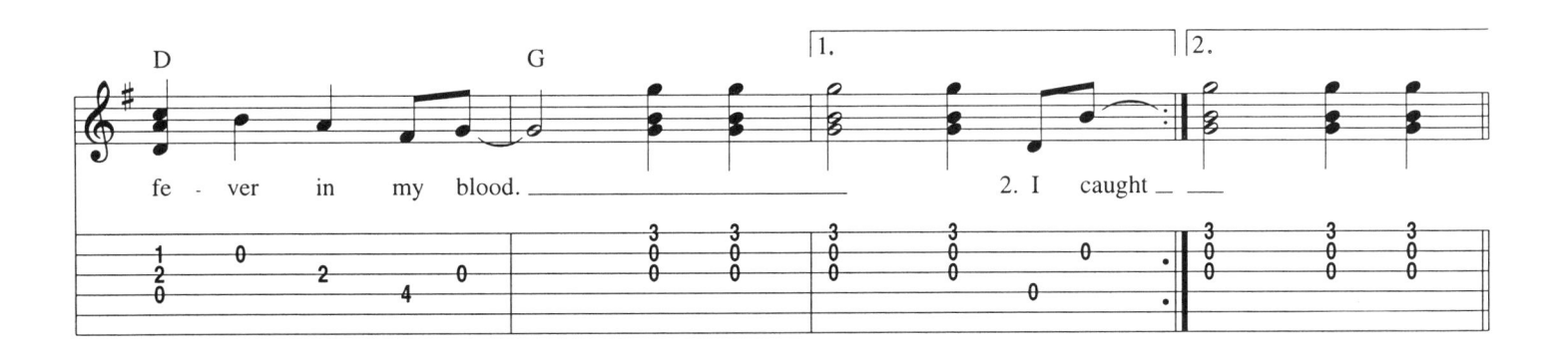

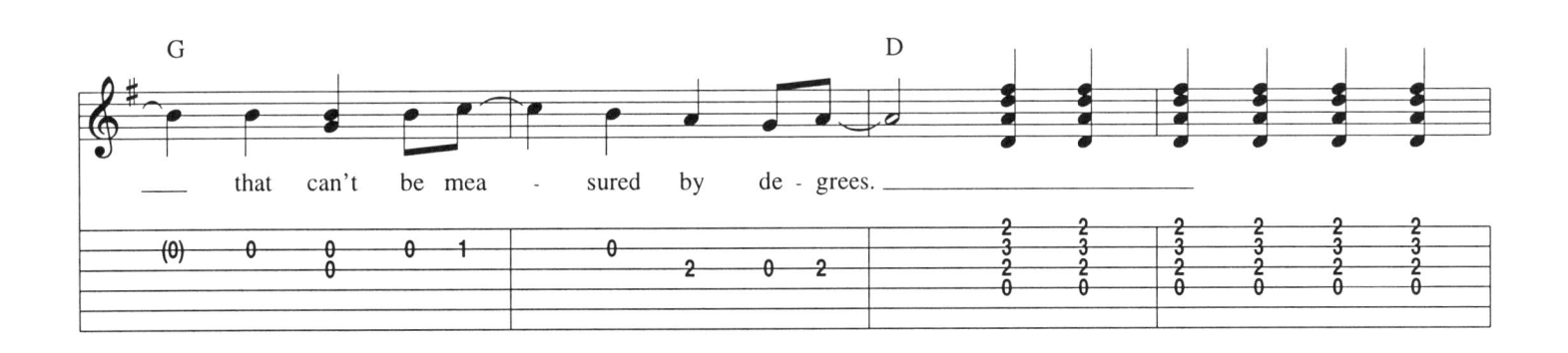

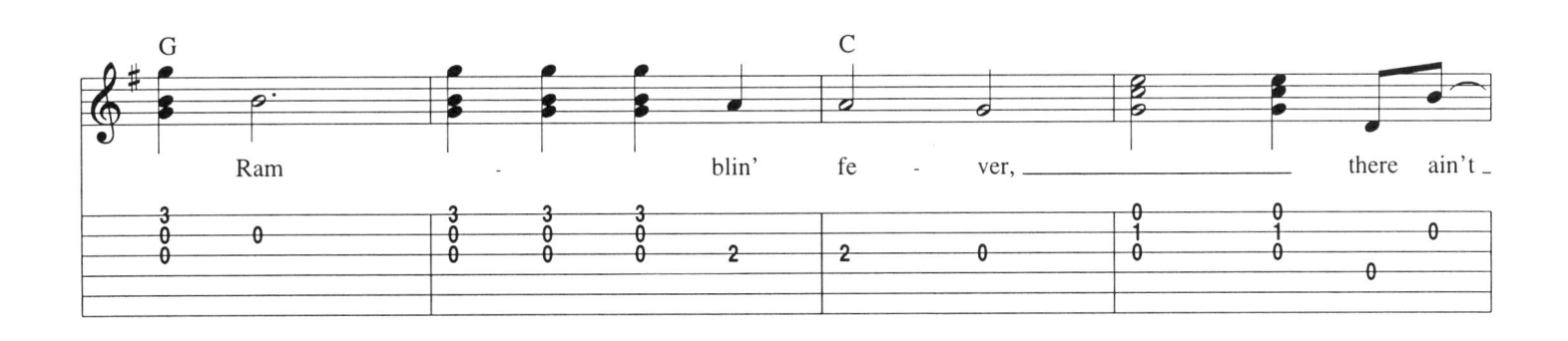

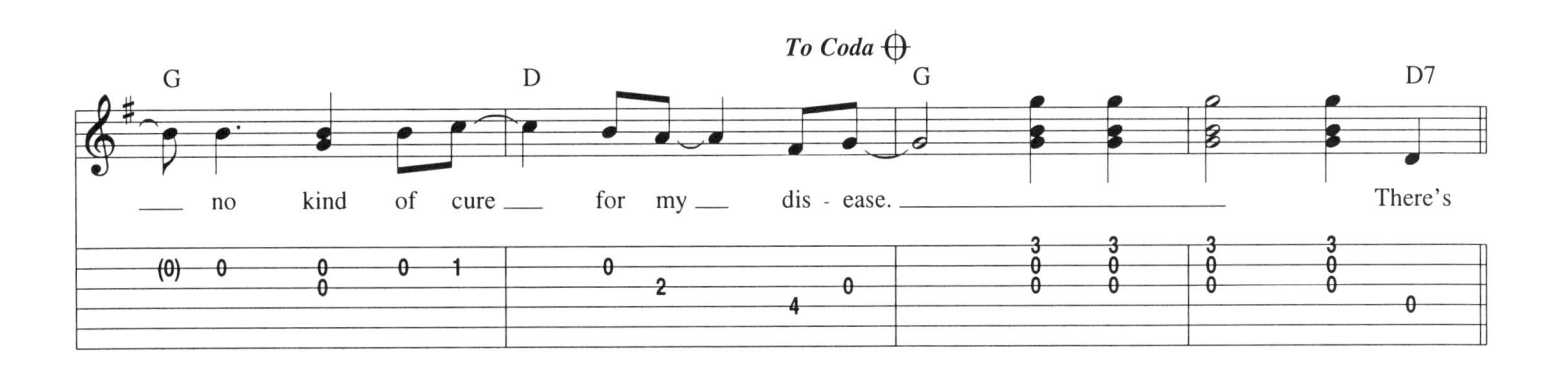

fe - ver in my blood. 2. I caught

Chorus
Ram - blin' fe - ver, the kind that can't be mea - sured by de - grees.

Ram - blin' fe - ver, there ain't no kind of cure for my dis - ease. There's

Bridge
G
C
times that I could bed down on a so - fa and
G
C
let some pret - ty la - dy rub my back and
Am
C
G
spend the ear - ly morn - ing drink - ing cof - fee and
D
G
talk - in' a - bout when I'll be com - in' back. 'Cause I
C
don't let no wom - an tie me down and I'll

Additional Lyrics

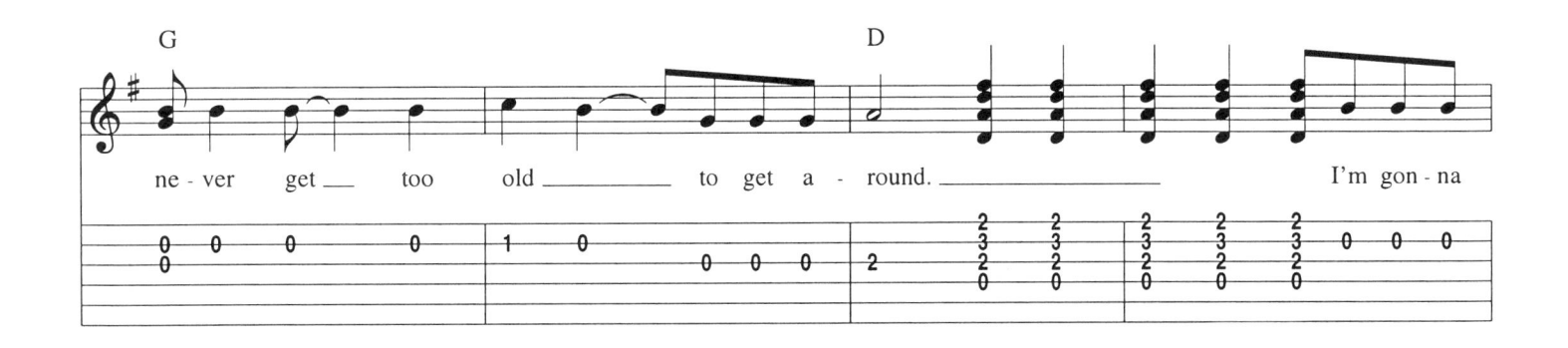

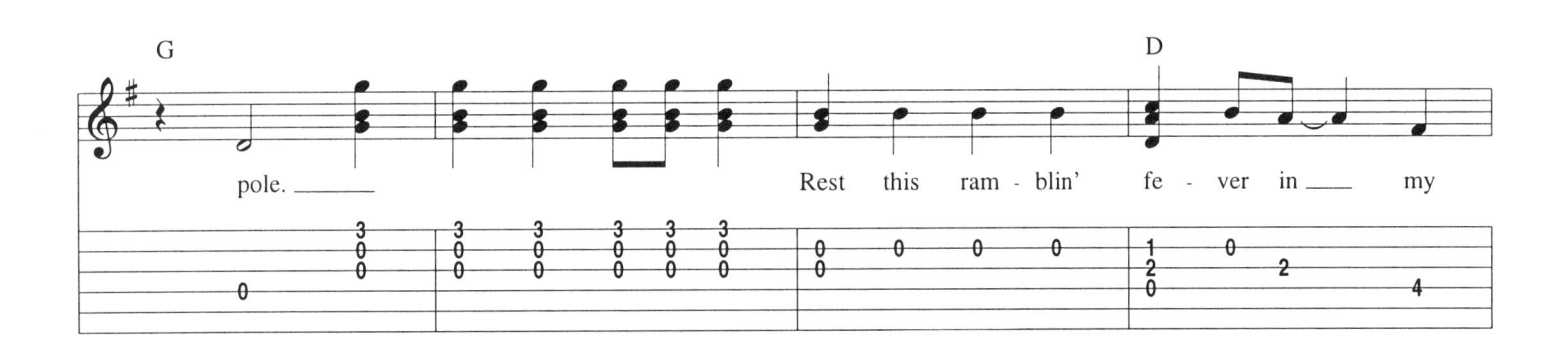

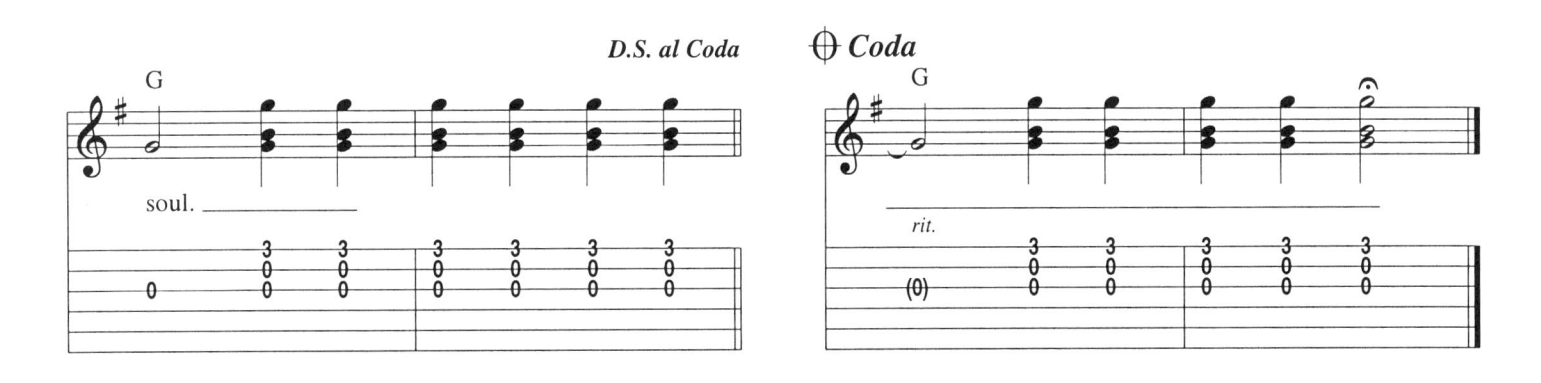

2. I caught this ramblin' fever long ago
   When I first heard a lonesome whistle blow.
   If someone said I ever gave a damn,
   They damn sure told you wrong.
   I've had ramblin' fever all along.

Reasons to Quit

Words and Music by Merle Haggard

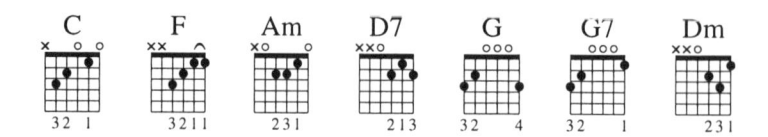

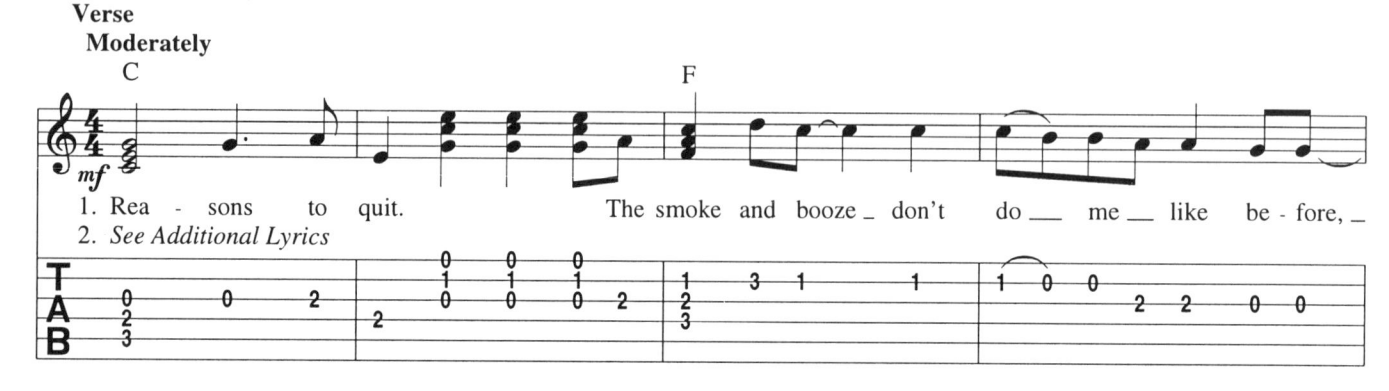

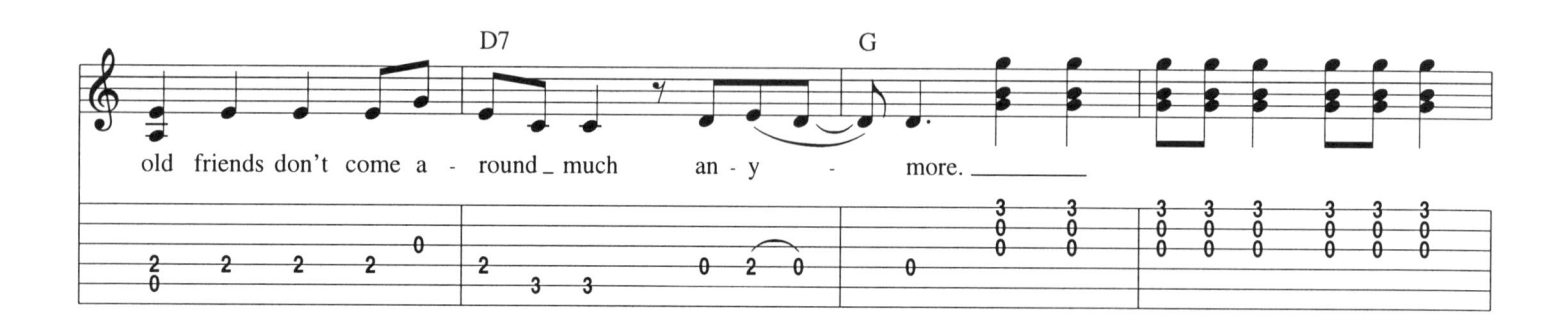

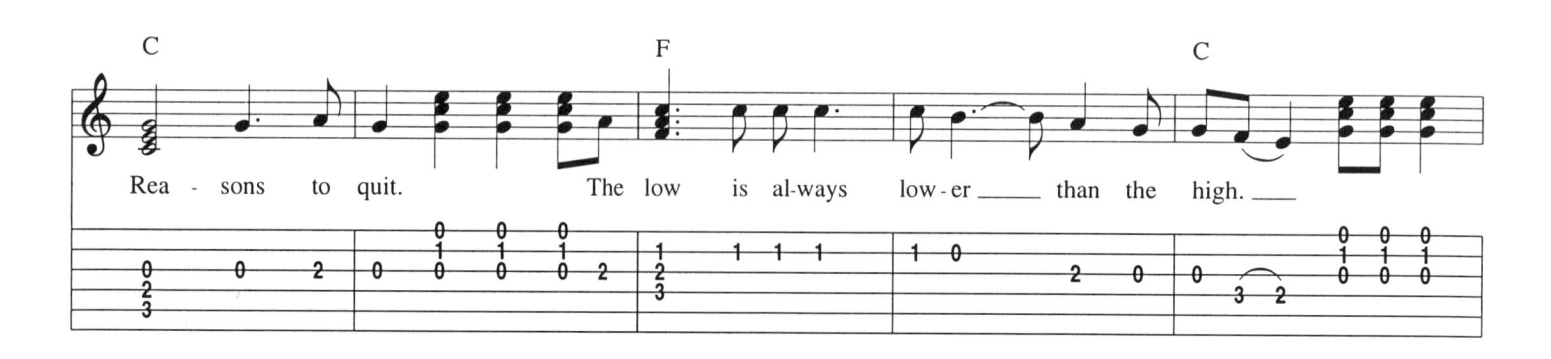

Chords: C, F, Am, D7, G, G7, Dm

Strum Pattern: 3, 4
Pick Pattern: 1, 3

Verse
Moderately

1. Rea - sons to quit. The smoke and booze don't do me like be - fore,
2. *See Additional Lyrics*

and I'm hard - ly ev - er so - ber, and my old friends don't come a - round much an - y - more.

Rea - sons to quit. The low is al - ways low - er than the high.

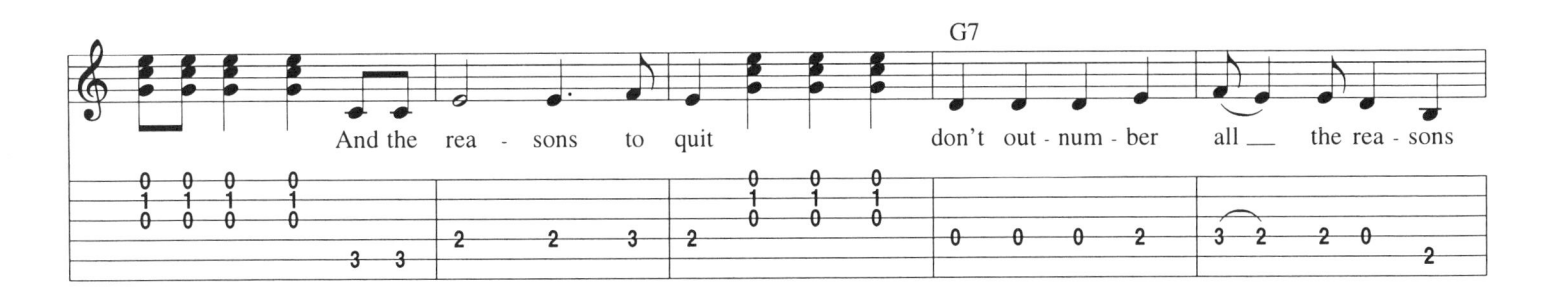

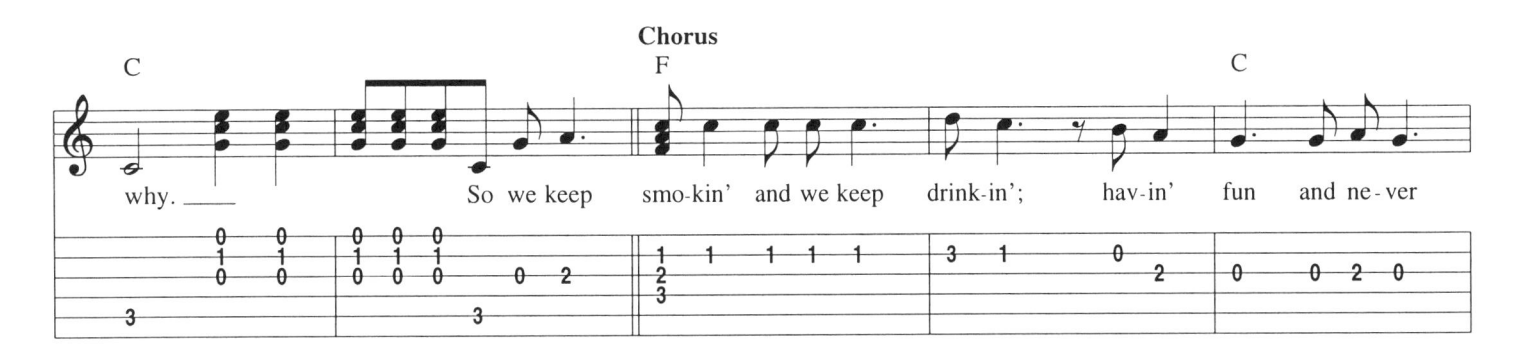

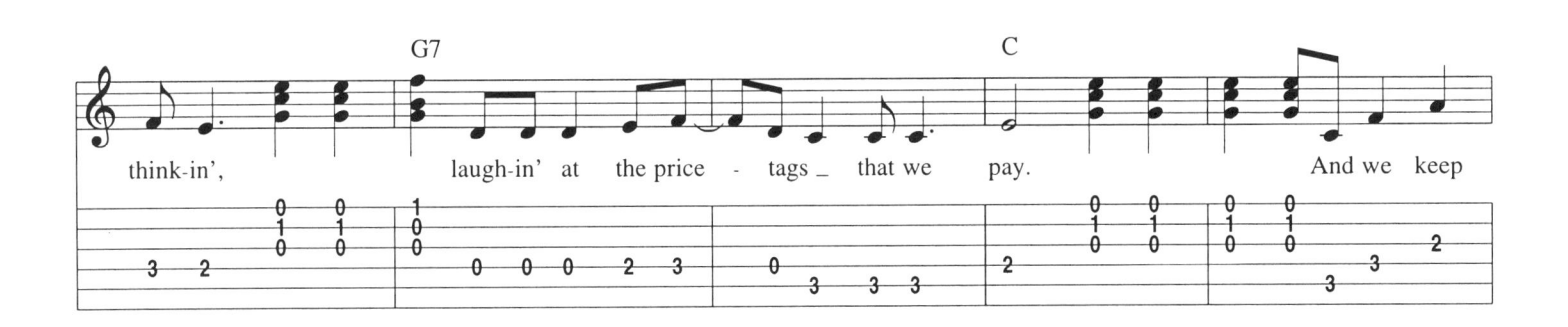

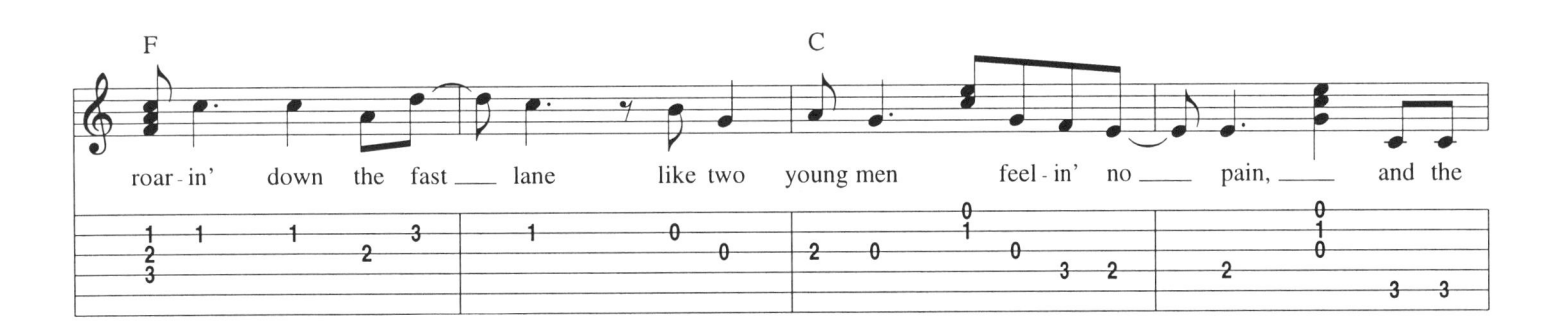

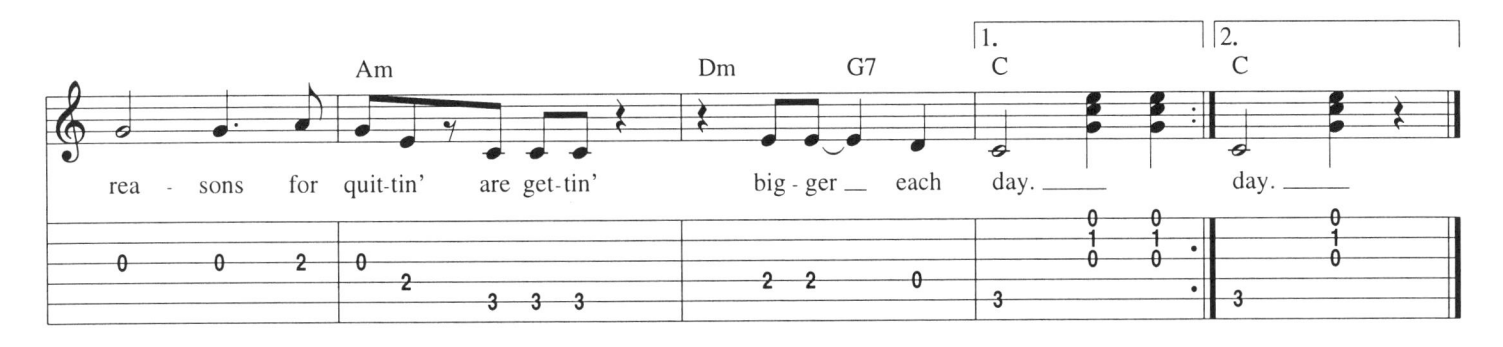

Additional Lyrics

2. Reasons to quit.
   I can't afford the habit all the time.
   I need to be sober,
   I need to write some new songs that will rhyme.
   Reasons to quit.
   They have no rhyme or reason when you're high.

Red Bandana

Words and Music by Merle Haggard

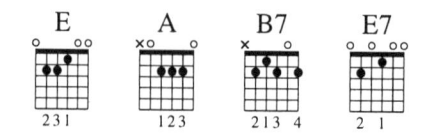

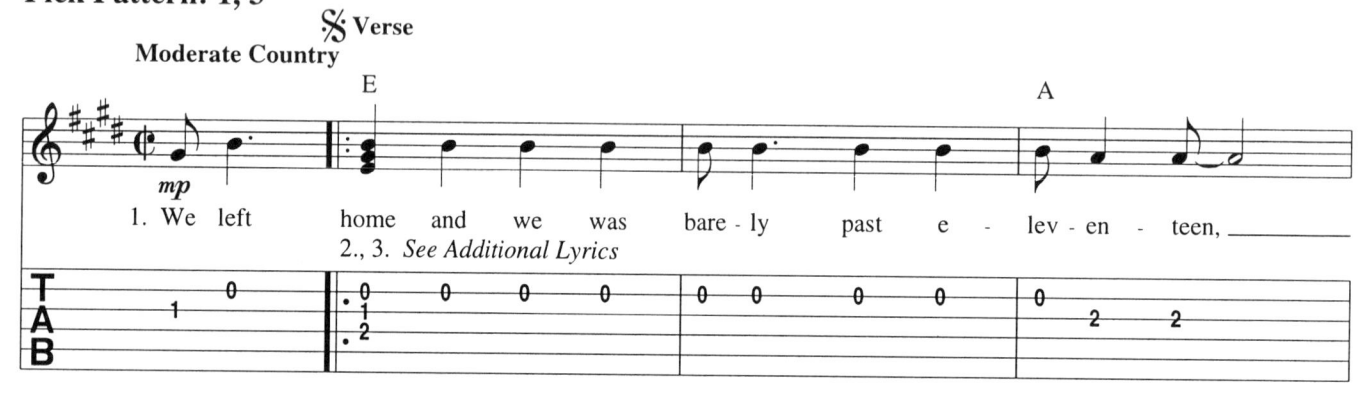

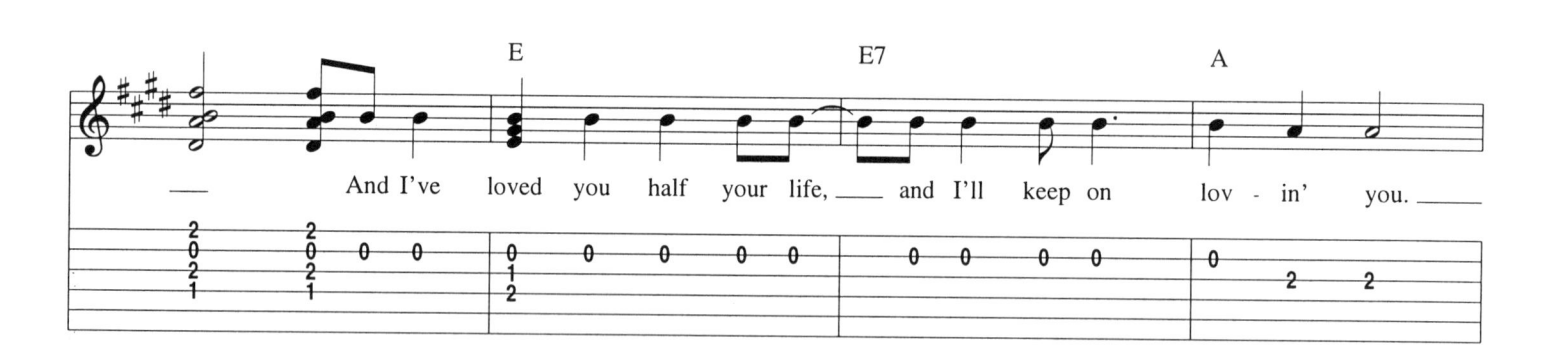

Chords: E, A, B7, E7

Strum Pattern: 3, 4
Pick Pattern: 1, 3

Moderate Country

Verse

1. We left home and we was barely past eleven,
2., 3. *See Additional Lyrics*

we've been back and forth and all around through hail and rain.

And I've loved you half your life, and I'll keep on lovin' you.

But I can't change and live the way you want me to. 2. We

Copyright © 1978 Sony/ATV Songs LLC
All Rights Administered by Sony/ATV Music Publishing, 8 Music Square West, Nashville, TN 37203
International Copyright Secured   All Rights Reserved

Additional Lyrics

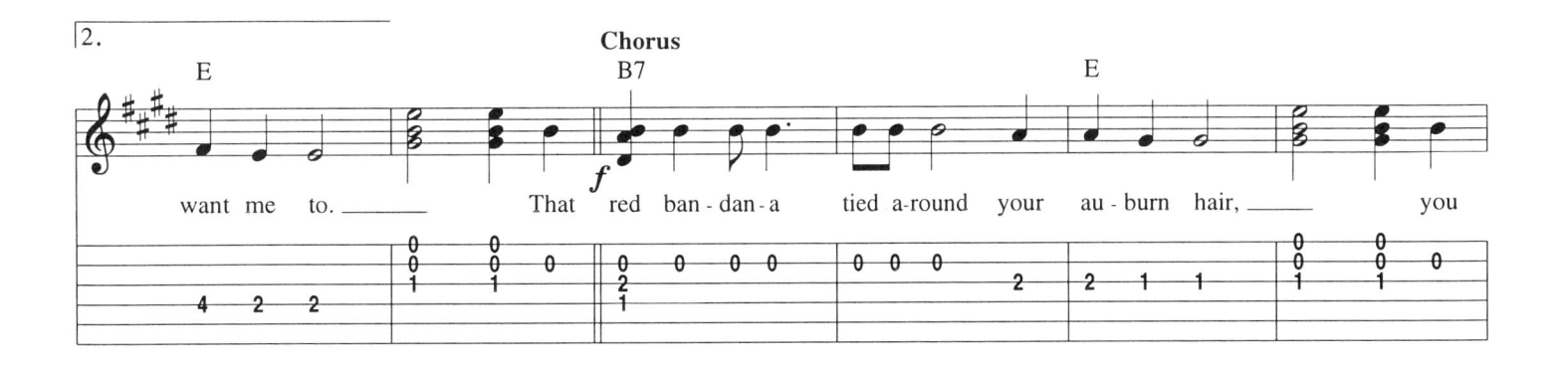

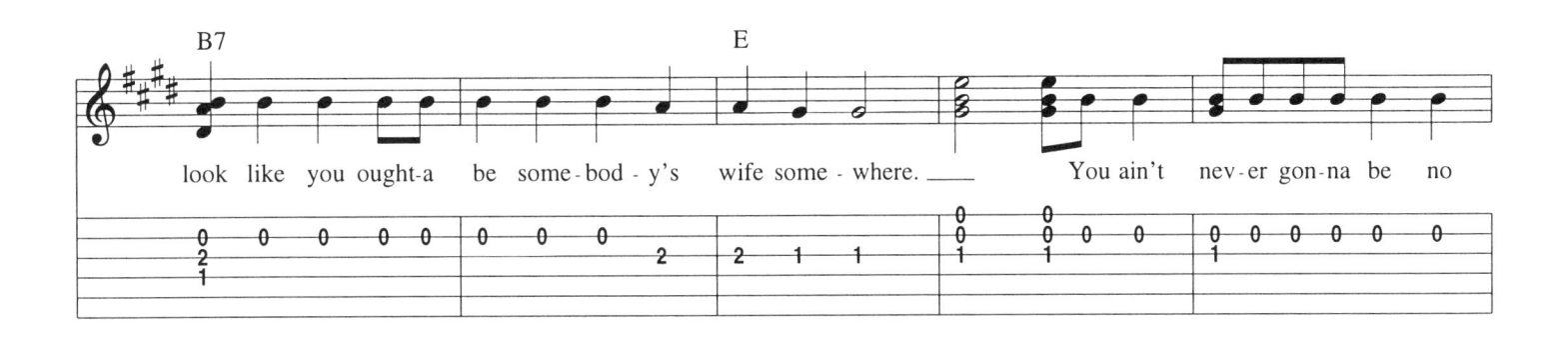

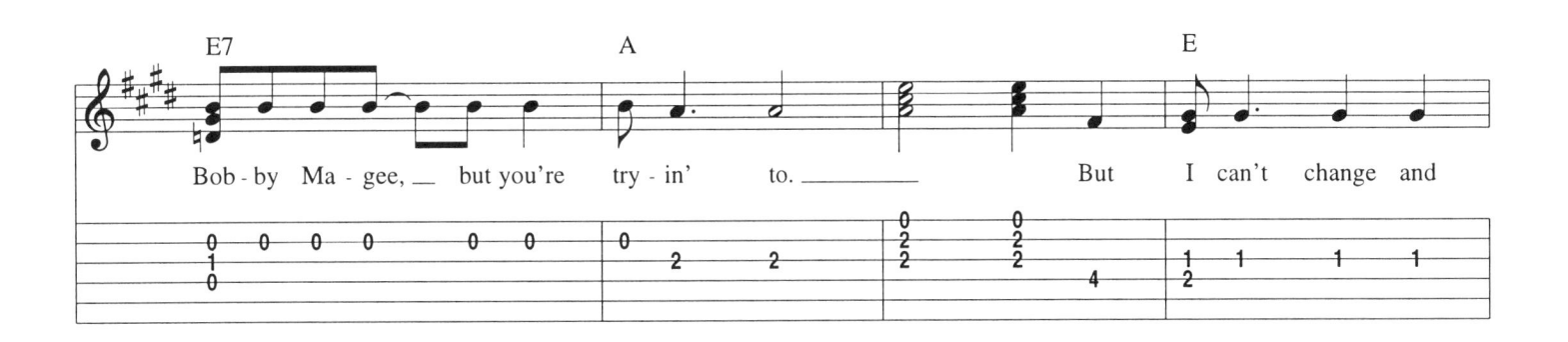

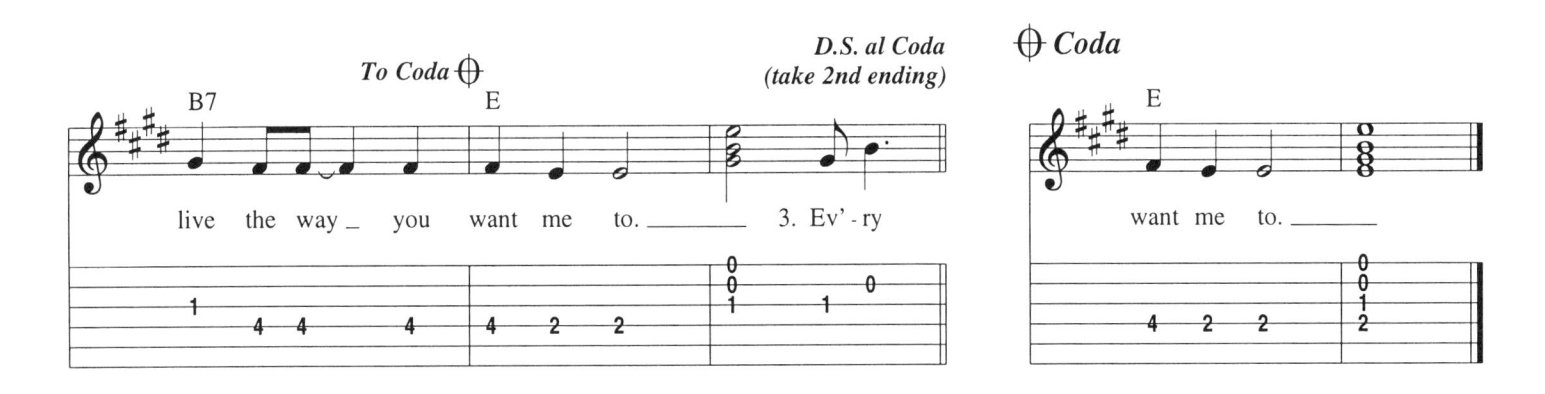

2. We spend a lot of time out on the highway,
   Comin' from some town we've played along the way.
   And after thirty years of knowin' me the way you do,
   You know I can't change and live the way you want me to.

3. Ev'ry time you leave the stage I know you've had your fill,
   And I wonder why you grew up and I never will.
   Hey, I'm forty-one today, still goin' on twenty-two,
   But I can't change and live the way you want me to.

Sing Me Back Home

Words and Music by Merle Haggard

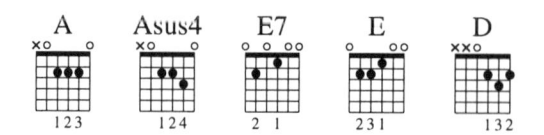

Chords used: A, Asus4, E7, E, D

Strum Pattern: 3, 4
Pick Pattern: 1, 3

Intro
Moderately

[Verse 1]
The war-den led a pris-'ner down a hall-way to his doom, and I stood up to say good-bye like all the rest. And I heard him tell the war-den, just be-fore he reached my cell, let my

2. *See Additional Lyrics*

Copyright © 1967 Sony/ATV Songs LLC
Copyright Renewed
All Rights Administered by Sony/ATV Music Publishing, 8 Music Square West, Nashville, TN 37203
International Copyright Secured   All Rights Reserved

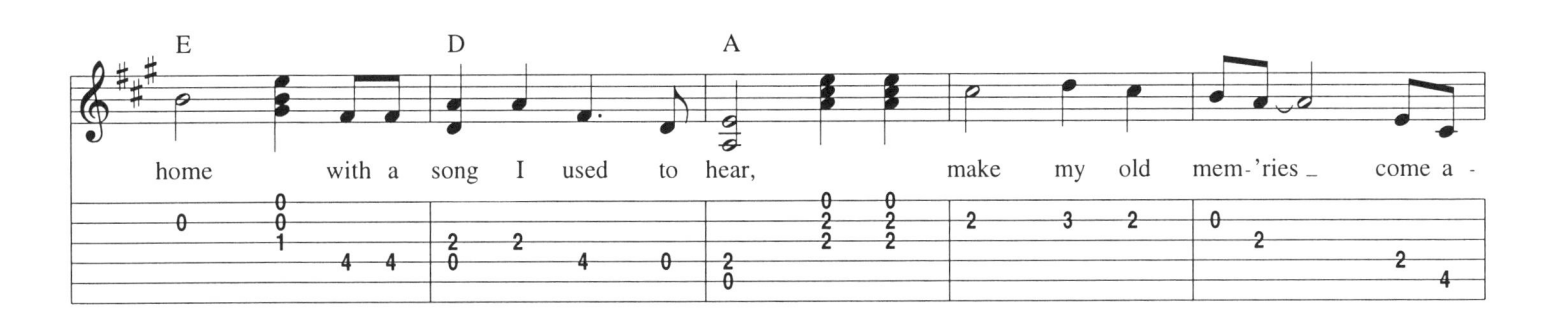

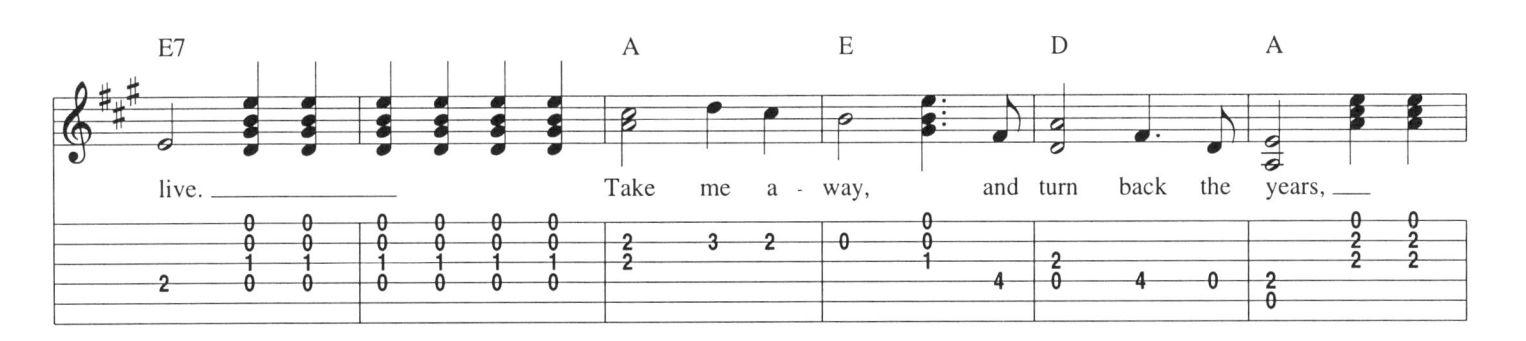

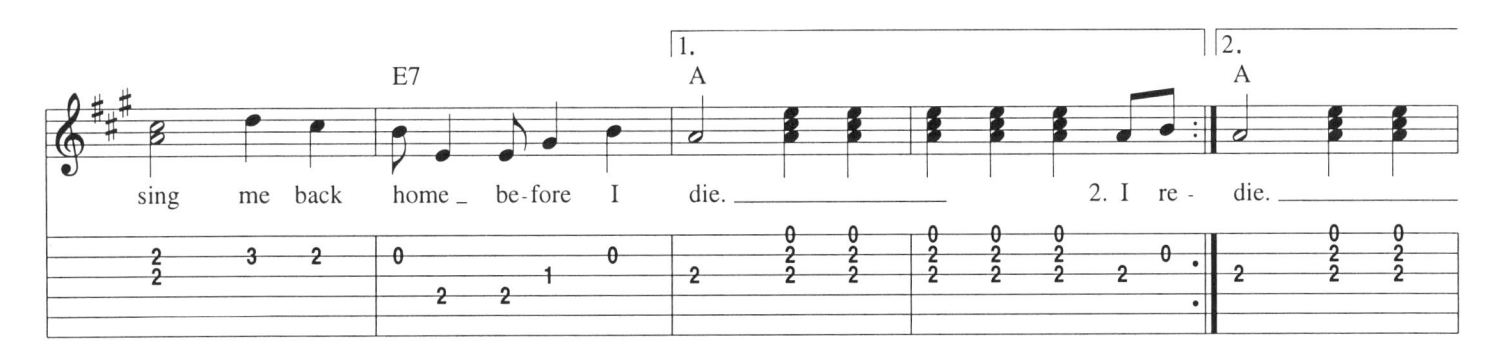

Additional Lyrics

2. I recall last Sunday morning
   A choir from off the street
   Came in to sing a few old gospel songs.
   And I heard him tell the singers,
   There's a song my mama sang,
   Could I hear it once before you move along.

Workin' Man Blues

Words and Music by Merle Haggard

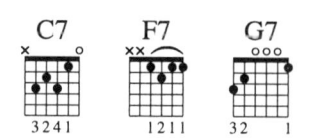

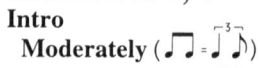

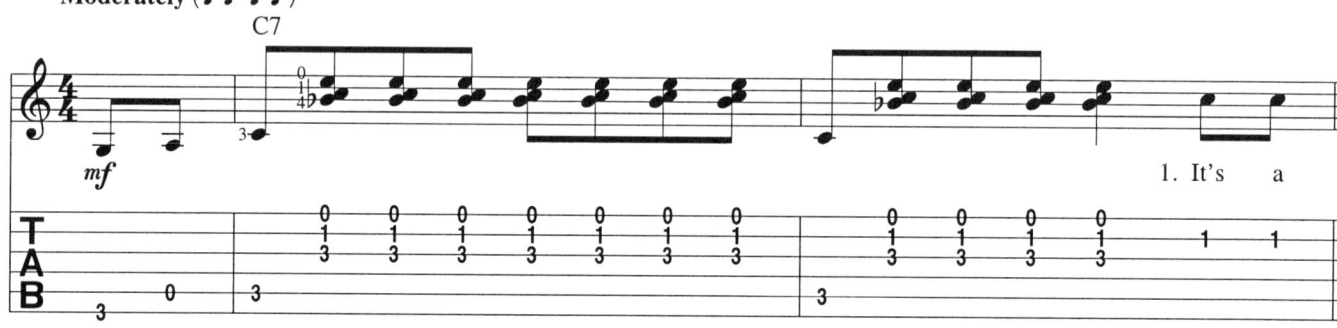

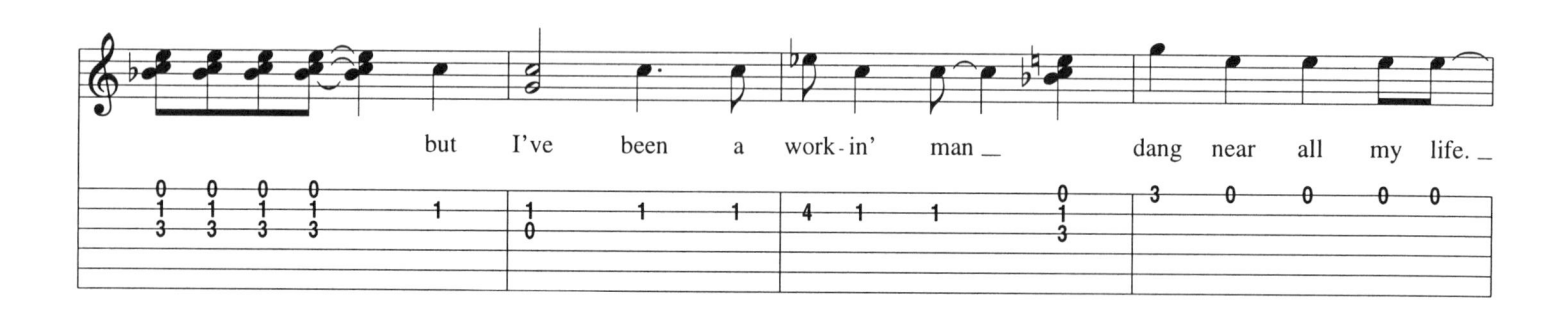

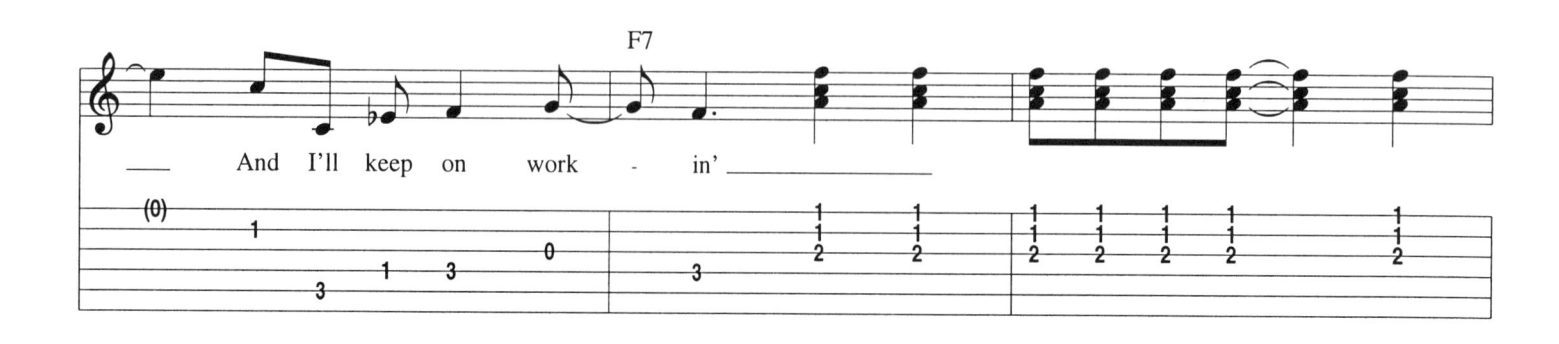

Chords: C7, F7, G7

Strum Pattern: 2, 3
Pick Pattern: 3, 4

Intro
Moderately

C7

1. It's a

Verse
C7

big job just get-tin' by ___ with nine kids ___ and a wife, ___

2., 3., 4. *See Additional Lyrics*

but I've been a work-in' man ___ dang near all my life. ___

F7

___ And I'll keep on work - in' ___

Copyright © 1969 Sony/ATV Songs LLC
Copyright Renewed
All Rights Administered by Sony/ATV Music Publishing, 8 Music Square West, Nashville, TN 37203
International Copyright Secured   All Rights Reserved

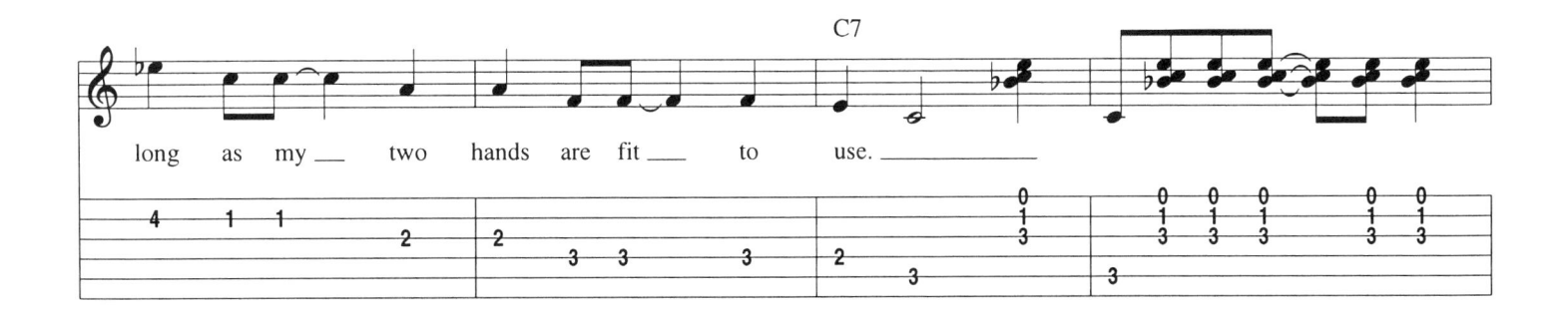

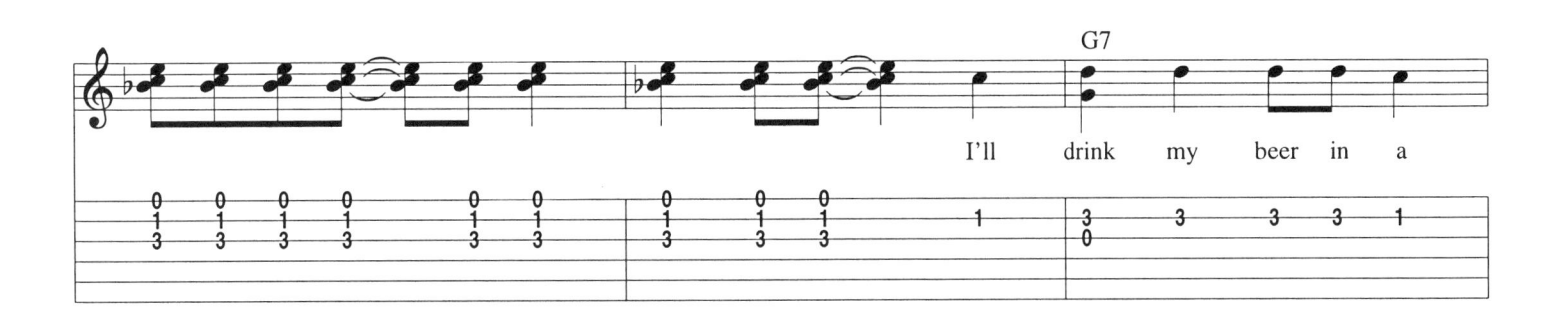

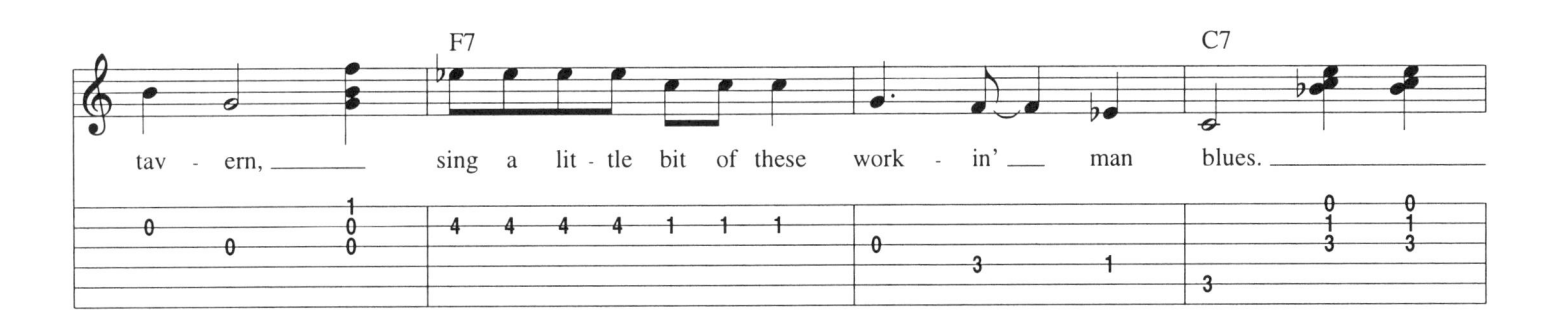

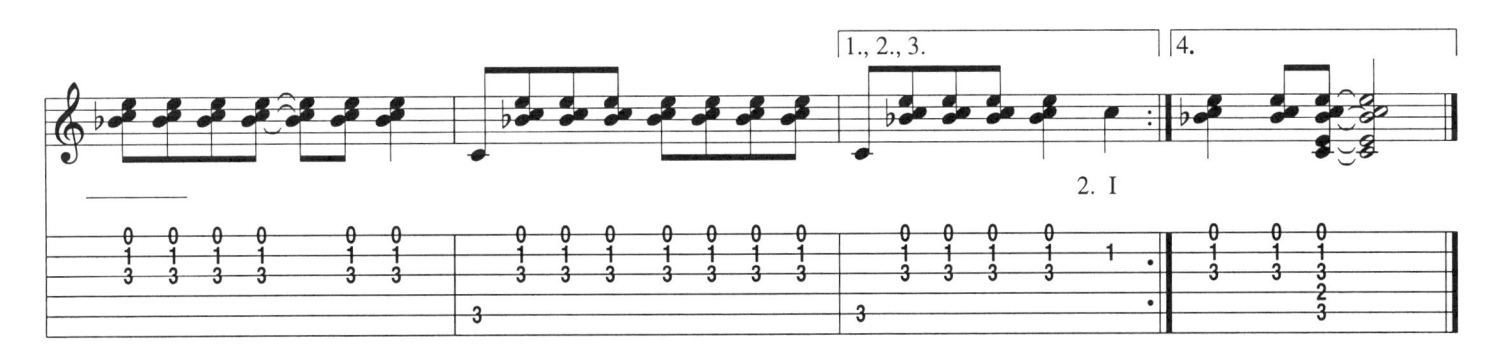

Additional Lyrics

2. I keep my nose on the grindstone, work hard everyday.
   I might get a little tired on the weekend, after I draw my pay.
   I'll go back workin', come Monday morning I'm right back with the crew.
   And I drink a little beer that evening,
   Sing a little bit of these workin' man blues.

3. Sometimes I think about leaving, do a little bumming around.
   I want to throw my bills out the window, catch a train to another town.
   I'll go back workin', gotta buy my kids a brand new pair of shoes.
   I drink a little beer in a tavern,
   Cry a little bit of these workin' man blues.

4. Well, Hey! Hey! The workin' man, the workin' man like me.
   I ain't never been on welfare, that's one place I won't be.
   I'll be workin', long as my two hands are fit to use.
   I'll drink my beer in a tavern,
   Sing a little bit of these workin' man blues.

You Take Me for Granted

Words and Music by Leona Williams

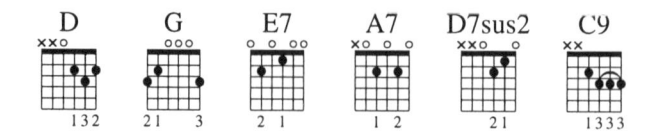

Strum Pattern: 8, 9
Pick Pattern: 8, 9

Verse
Moderate Country Waltz

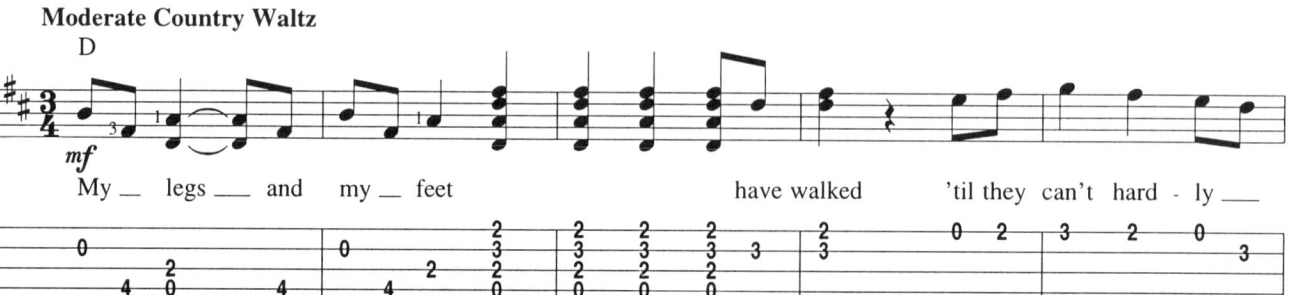

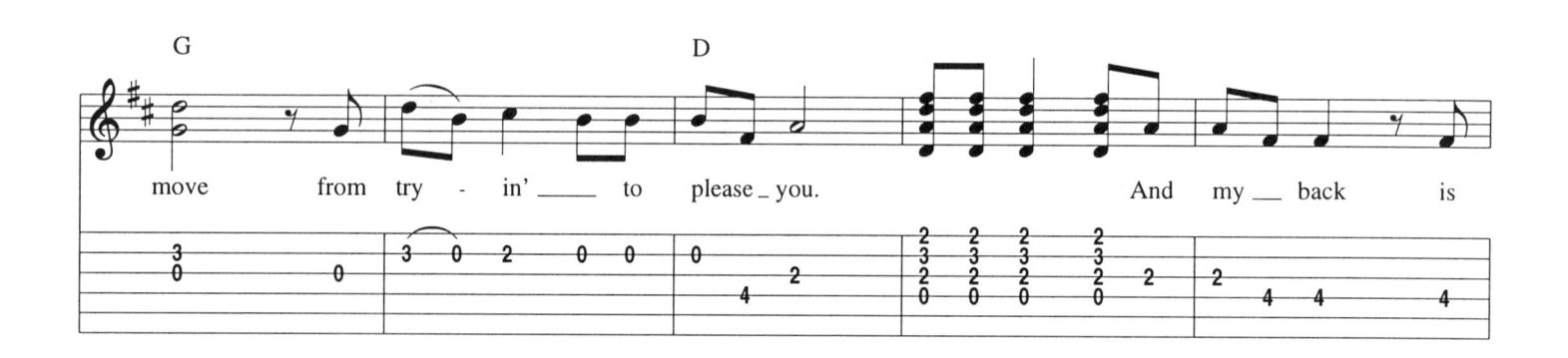

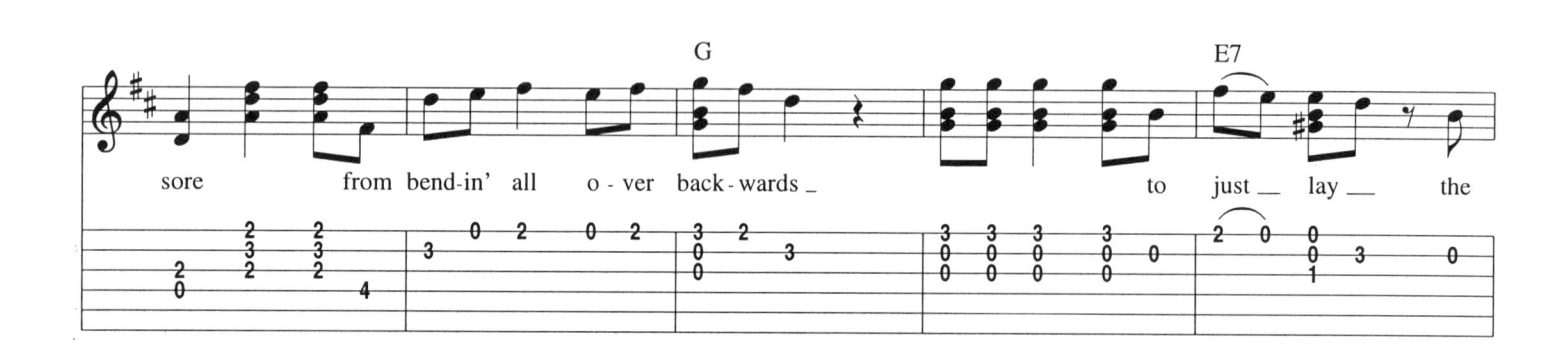

My legs and my feet have walked 'til they can't hardly move from tryin' to please you. And my back is sore from bendin' all over backwards to just lay the world at your door. I've tried so hard to keep a smile on a sad face while deep down it's break-in' my heart. And as sure as the

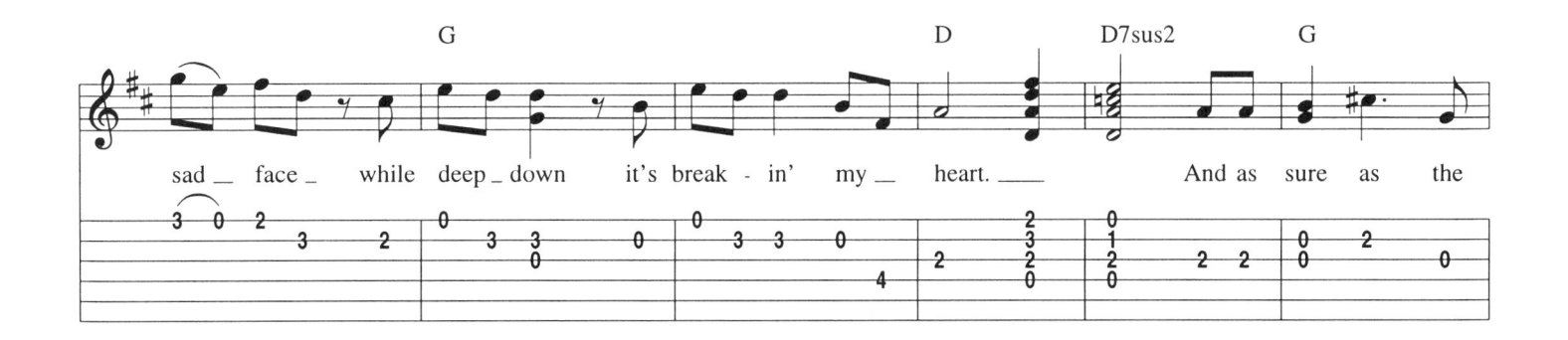

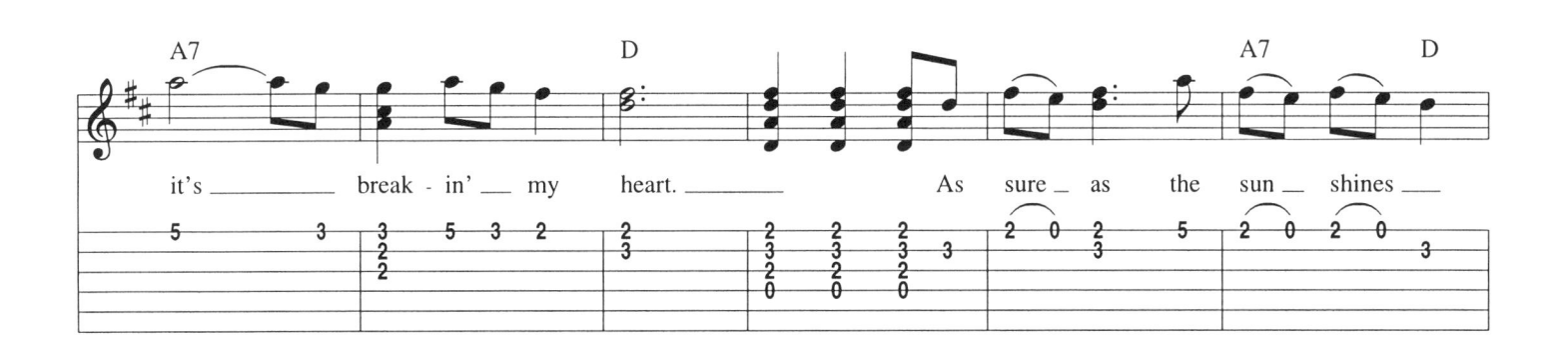

sun shines I'll be a life-time not know-in' if I've done my

Chorus

part. 'Cause you take me for grant-ed and

it's break-in' my heart. As sure as the sun shines

I'll be a life-time not know-in' if I've done my part.

Twinkle Twinkle Lucky Star

Words and Music by Merle Haggard

Strum Pattern: 8
Pick Pattern: 8

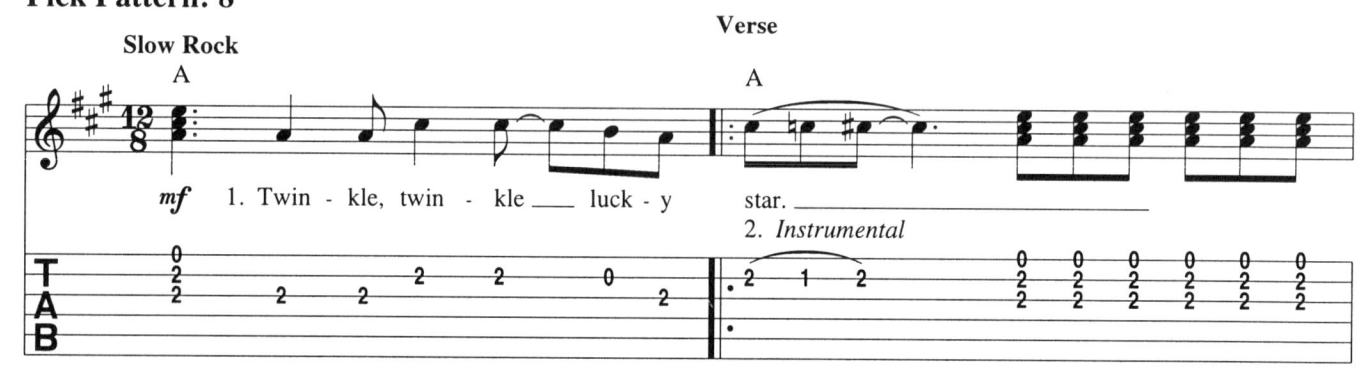

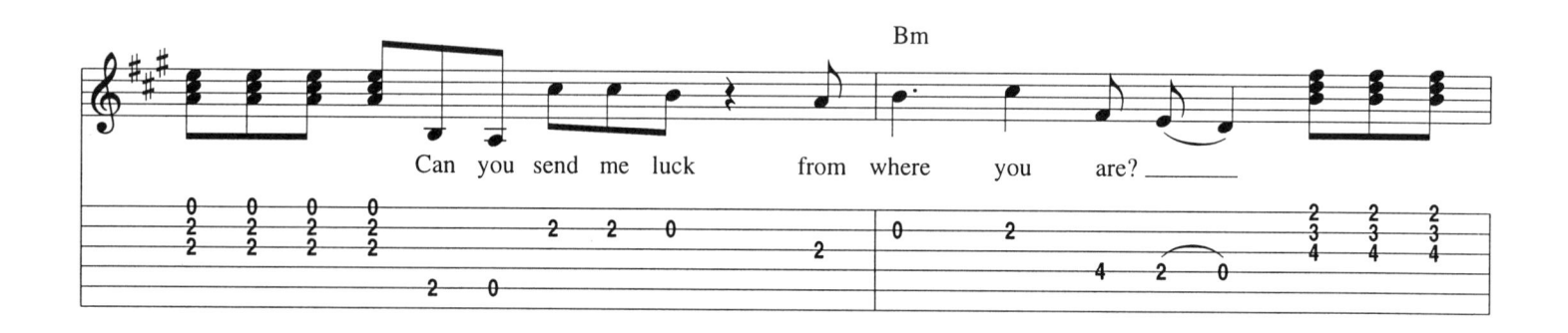

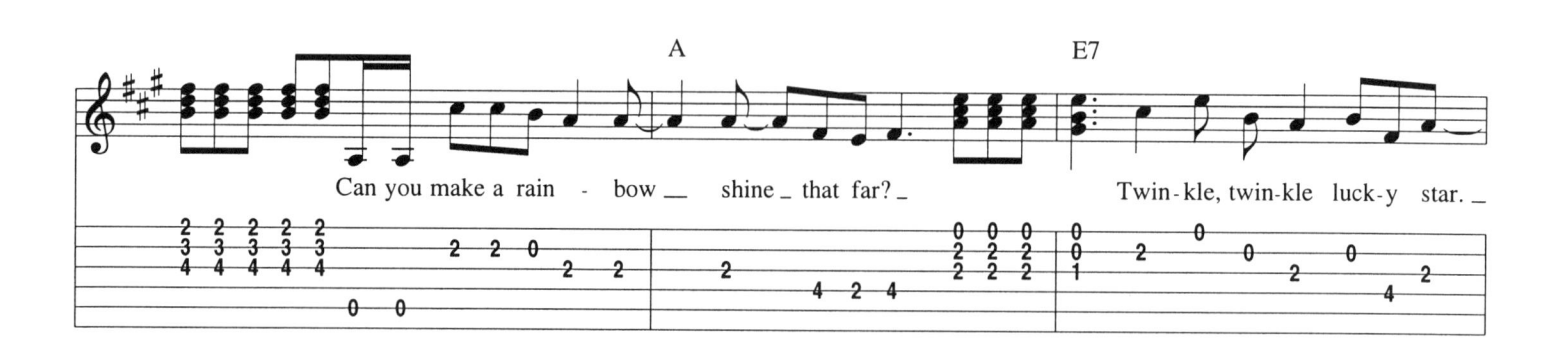

Slow Rock

Verse

1. Twin-kle, twin-kle ___ luck-y star. ___
2. Instrumental

Can you send me luck from where you are? ___

Can you make a rain-bow ___ shine ___ that far? ___ Twin-kle, twin-kle luck-y star. ___

Can you real-ly make a wish come ___ true? ___

Copyright © 1988 Sony/ATV Songs LLC
All Rights Administered by Sony/ATV Music Publishing, 8 Music Square West, Nashville, TN 37203
International Copyright Secured   All Rights Reserved

Bm
Do you shine on just a cho - sen few?
A
Is it o - ver? Have I gone too far?
E7 A D A
Twin - kle, twin - kle luck - y star.
Like two
Chorus
E7 A
ships on the o - cean we drift - ed a - part
E7 A
and you found an is - land at sea.

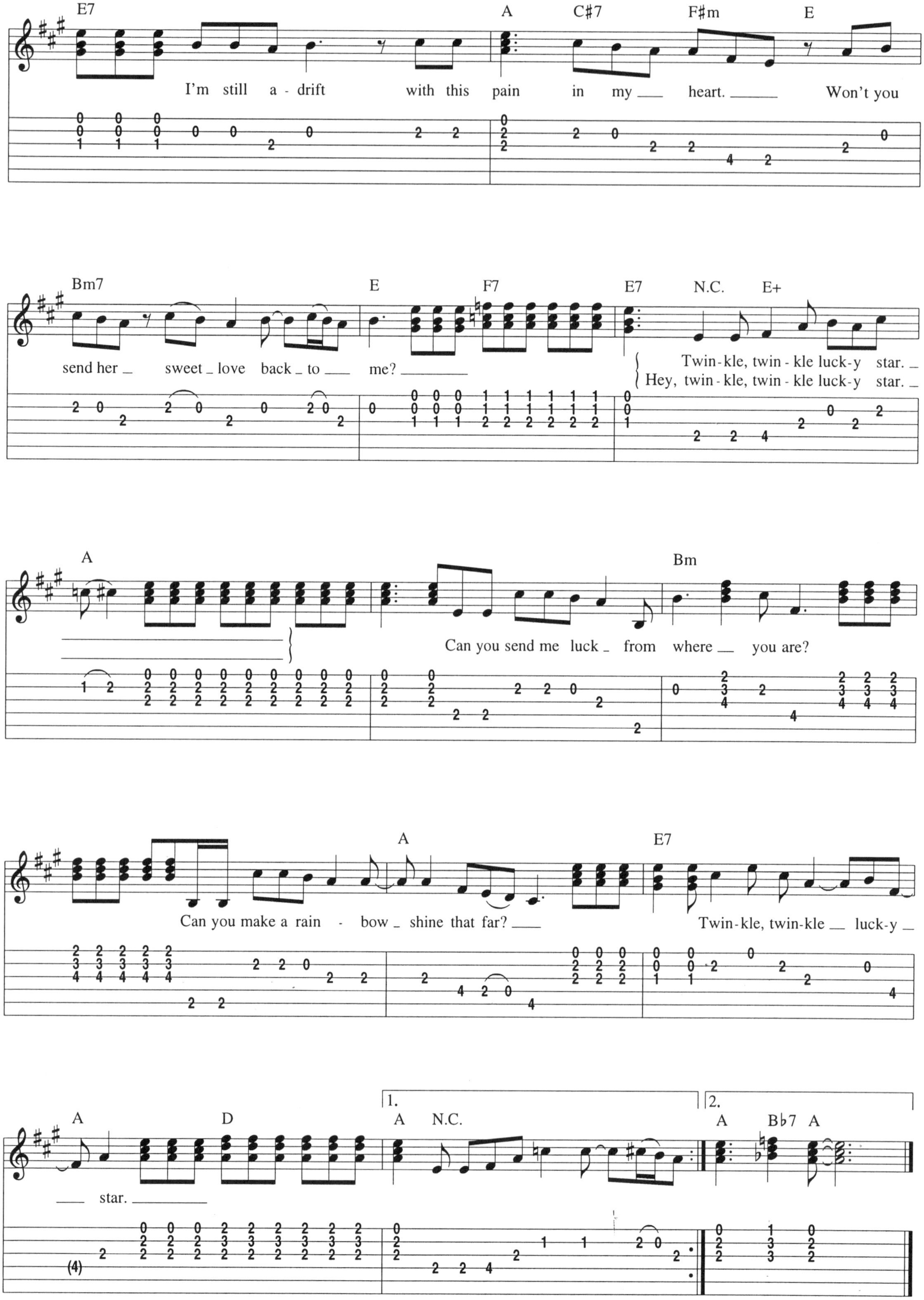
E7 A C#7 F#m E
I'm still a - drift with this pain in my heart. Won't you
Bm7 E F7 E7 N.C. E+
send her sweet love back to me?
Twin-kle, twin-kle luck-y star.
Hey, twin-kle, twin-kle luck-y star.
A Bm
Can you send me luck from where you are?
A E7
Can you make a rain - bow shine that far?
Twin-kle, twin-kle luck-y
A D
star.
1. A N.C.
2. A B♭7 A